The Struggle
for Afghanistan

Also by Richard S. Newell

The Politics of Afghanistan

The Struggle for Afghanistan

Nancy Peabody Newell
Richard S. Newell

Cornell University Press

Ithaca and London

First published 1981 by Cornell University Press.
Published in the United Kingdom by Cornell University Press Ltd., Ely House, 37 Dover Street, London W1X 4HQ.

First printing, Cornell Paperbacks, 1982.

International Standard Book Number (cloth) 0-8014-1389-3
International Standard Book Number (paper) 0-8014-9236-X
Library of Congress Catalog Card Number 80-69829
Printed in the United States of America

The paper in this book is acid-free, and meets the guidelines for permanence and durability of the Committee on Production Guidelines for Book Longevity of the Council on Library Resources.

*To the people of Afghanistan,
whose courage in a struggle against
overwhelming odds is an inspiration
in a world increasingly given to
cynicism and doubt*

Contents

A Note from the Authors   11
Acknowledgments   16

1. The People and Their Land   19
2. The Rise and Fall of the Afghan Monarchy   34
3. Marxism in Afghanistan   53
4. The Khalq Regime, April 27, 1978–December 27, 1979   66
5. The Resistance   91
6. The Soviet Invasion of December 1979   107
7. The Struggle for Afghanistan   129
8. A New Era of Crisis   190

Appendix 1. Resolutions on Afghanistan Adopted
    January 28, 1980, at the Extraordinary Meeting of
    the Foreign Ministers of the Islamic Conference   217
Appendix 2. Resolutions on Afghanistan Adopted
    May 22, 1980, by the Conference of Islamic
    Foreign Ministers   219
Notes   221
Index   229

Illustrations

Pushtun man, Samangan	24
A *buzkashi* game near Kabul	26
Hazara women and children, Hazarajat	27
Nomad and daughter, Jalalabad	29
Farmer, Bamiyan	32
Mother and child, Bamiyan	82
Nuristani man, Faizabad	97
The Kunar Valley	99
Faizabad, from across the Kokcha River	102
Turkoman woman, Samangan	133
The Khyber Pass	135
The east side of Kabul, from Sher Darwaza Mountain	142
The village of Abdar, in the Panjshir Valley	146
The Kunduz Valley	148
Men praying at the entrance to a mosque in Istalif, near Kabul	150
East meets West in Jalalabad	156
A walled section of Ghazni	160
Boy with melon, Bamiyan	164
Girl, Bamiyan	165
A *qala* (fortress home) in the Logar Valley	166
The Kohdaman Valley, from Istalif	168
Hunter, Panjshir Valley	169
A teahouse in Kabul	171
Students of Rabia Balkhi Lycée, Kabul	175
Father and son, Kabul Gorge	177

Illustrations

Darulaman Palace, near Kabul   179
Bamiyan countryside, from Shar-i-Gholghola   181
The Shikari Valley, near Bamiyan   186

Map of Afghanistan   20–21

10

A Note from
the Authors

My spirit will remain in Afghanistan, though my soul will go to
God. My last words to you, my son and successor, are: Never
trust the Russians.

—Abd ur-Rahman Khan
(d. 1901)

We wrote this book when it became obvious that the noncommunist world was greatly concerned about the Afghan crisis but
very little concerned about Afghanistan. Afghanistan was immediately seen as a victim; Soviet control was conceded from the
beginning. As many other victims have found before, the violation was an irritant. The slaughter of Afghans was seen to
threaten world peace, disturb détente, and endanger access to
Middle East oil. In the torrent of words that has flowed since the
crisis began, few have been directed at the plight of the Afghans
themselves.

We are convinced that this neglect is to a large degree responsible for the failure of the world community to respond
effectively to the Soviet invasion. The crux of the matter is that a
large nation has attempted to take away the independence of a
small nation by force. That should have made the Afghan cause
universal. Yet it has been treated as hopeless. Afghan resistance
is even perceived as endangering Iran and Pakistan because it
may induce the Soviet government to pour in more troops, who
may cross borders in "hot pursuit."

Such assessments fail to recognize that Soviet control over

Afghanistan is not an established fact. Afghan-resistance has been the only response from any quarter which has had a directly punishing effect on the Soviet Union. Support of the Afghan struggle remains by far the most effective means of reversing the process unleashed by the invasion. The continued struggle of the Afghan people is in effect a struggle on behalf of their region, the viability of the international oil market, and the maintenance of the fragile structure of world peace. Outside assistance is therefore vital not only to the Afghans but to anyone who opposes Soviet expansionism.

Effective support of Afghanistan's liberation struggle requires an understanding of why and how the Afghans have become embroiled in this crisis. To provide such an understanding has been our purpose in writing this book. It offers a short overview for the general reader, not a definitive treatment of the subject (which in any case cannot be written at this time). It attempts to put Afghanistan in its proper place in the geopolitical puzzle, but its main emphasis is on the tragedy of Afghanistan's loss of independence and the struggle of its people to regain it.

More than anything else the invasion has exposed the Soviet government as an aggressor. It was carried out in the name of the Brezhnev Doctrine, which declares that once a nation becomes part of the Soviet bloc, it cannot leave. While the USSR had already demonstrated its willingness to enforce that doctrine in Europe—in Hungary in 1956, in Czechoslovakia in 1968—this is the first time it has done so in Asia.

There is no Asian counterpart to the painfully drawn lines of the East European satellite zone (the Iron Curtain) which Stalin insisted on establishing after World War II. The primary thrust of Soviet foreign policy in Asia has been directed toward the development of friendly relations with noncommunist governments through diplomacy and assistance. In attacking the Afghan people, the Soviet Union has adopted a new method of dealing with Asians. The invasion has also shown the bankruptcy of American policy in regard to Asia. The invasion has demonstrated the weakness and disunity of Asian and Muslim countries in the face of Soviet aggression. The invasion has demonstrated the willingness of Western Europe to overlook Soviet aggression elsewhere as long as it continues to benefit from détente. The invasion has dramatized the defenselessness of the Middle East, the world's major source of oil. More than anything else, the invasion proves once again that the security of nations is indivisible. Unchallenged aggression against one, no matter how poor and remote, threatens all. As the democratic nations paid dearly in the 1940s for their failure to support the Spanish people in their struggle against fascism, those nations today risk their peace and security by their failure to support the Afghan people in their struggle against communist aggression.

There can be no question that it was an invasion. When Afghanistan's president, Hafizullah Amin, defied the Soviets, they eliminated him and brought in six divisions. The Soviets' claim that they answered a plea for help from the Afghan government suffers from the fundamental weakness of coming after the fact. A Soviet airborne unit had already made sure that Amin was dead before the "call" for Soviet troops was made.

The invasion cannot be disguised by the argument that the Soviets were already in control. If they had been in control, they would have had no need to make such a violent military move. Amin was not their man; he had seized power against their wishes. The invasion was mounted not to reinforce Soviet control but to establish it. It changed the USSR's role from that of a foreign guarantor of the government to that of the governing power itself. Amin's replacement, Babrak Karmal, and the government he heads are extensions of Soviet power now installed in Afghanistan.

The motives behind the Soviet move have been widely debated. Disagreement about those motives is the most striking feature of the international reaction to the invasion. None of the nations that have denounced the invasion was actually prepared to do anything effective about it. Almost all, including the United States, appear to have been caught off guard. The steps they took and the criticisms they voiced in response to the invasion have had no substantial impact on Soviet behavior. Their confusion and impotence indicate that they had not anticipated the Soviet move and could not grasp what the seizure of Afghanistan would mean.

Afghanistan's poverty and perceived remoteness contributed to the confusion. Why should the Soviets, or anyone else, want such a country? Its people presented almost no threat to anyone, certainly none to the Soviet Union. Its economy was backward; it had virtually no industry; its international trade was too limited to be coveted. Its isolation, poverty, and defenselessness prompted the United States, even at the height of the cold war, to deny Afghanistan military aid. For a quarter century the Kremlin had had no competitor in its domination of Afghanistan's foreign policy. The invasion merely sought to bring to a conclusion a process that had already engulfed a small nation whose fate appeared to be irrelevant to the rest of the world community. In view of the resentments the invasion was sure to cause, what did the USSR have to gain? Now that Soviet forces are there, an answer becomes obvious. Afghanistan itself offers little to the Soviets, but control over it critically alters the political, geostrategic, and psychological balance of forces in South Asia, the Indian Ocean, and the Middle East. Soviet control of Afghanistan exposes the region to pressures that imperil its unstable governments and leave other industrial powers at a serious disadvantage in the competition for influence and mineral resources, especially oil. Having discounted Afghanistan's importance and tacitly conceded the country to the Soviet bloc, the United States and its allies now find themselves reduced to gestures and symbolic acts in their scramble to salvage what is left of their position in Southwest Asia.

This calamity has been sprung like a magician's sleight of hand, so suddenly that appreciation of it has been slow to register. Soviet control of Afghanistan means there is no credible defense of the Persian Gulf.

Misjudgment of Soviet intentions toward Afghanistan is at the root of this calamity. One need not believe that the Russians have been obsessed by Peter the Great's dream of reaching the warm waters of the Indian Ocean to conclude that the Soviet Union has had designs on Afghanistan since the Bolsheviks set up their Central Asian republics in the 1920s. In playing the "Great Game" the Russians have taken a much longer view than their Western counterparts. After Khrushchev's visit to Afghanistan in 1955, the Soviets glossed over their growing presence there with elaborate propaganda and diplomatic charades that heralded the sovereignty and nonalignment of small Third World nations. They appeared to applaud Afghanistan's attempt to develop its natural and human resources through the aid of many nations. Their pose lured both anti-Soviet and nonaligned governments—and most of us who write on Afghanistan—into believing that they considered their best interests in the country to be served by a true and open nonalignment. Some effort was required to reconcile this stance with Afghanistan's all but total dependence on Soviet military aid. The friends the Soviets were winning in the Third World by their generosity to Afghanistan seemed well worth the cost. Pious hopes fed the conviction that the Soviets were satisfied with influence instead of control.

The conviction that the Soviets presented no threat to Afghanistan greatly simplified strategic thinking by Asians, Americans, and others concerning the vulnerability of the Middle East and South Asia to pressure from the north. Now that such thinking has been proved to have been wishful, the hard implications of having been wrong must be faced.

N. P. N.
R. S. N.

Cedar Falls, Iowa

Acknowledgments

We wish to acknowledge our debt to the people and institutions who helped to make this book possible. They include our typists, Judy Dohlman, Ann Risvedt, and Lois Jerke, who often worked under a good deal of pressure to finish the manuscript. Much of our most vital information was furnished by Mary Ann Sigfried, of the Afghanistan Council of the Asia Society of New York City, and by the Center for Afghanistan Studies of the University of Nebraska at Omaha. Information and advice have come from a number of Afghan friends who wish to remain anonymous. As is apparent in Chapter 7, we owe much to the press correspondents who have been courageous and clever enough to bring back reports on the fighting inside Afghanistan. We are particularly grateful to Barbara Burnham and Barbara Salazar of Cornell University Press for their intelligent guidance, patience, and humor in seeing us through this project. Noel Newell-Williams improved the index.

All but four of the photographs are part of the superb collection made by William Witt. He and his wife, Sandy, were Peace Corps volunteers in Afghanistan from 1973 to 1975. The photographs on pages 27 and 160 were taken by Nancy Peabody Newell; those on pages 142 and 148 were taken by Richard S. Newell.

Our family and friends have given us crucial support. We thank them especially for their encouragement. They were right, it can be done.

The Struggle
for Afghanistan

1

The People
and Their Land

Few people have been more distinctively shaped by their land
and its location than have the Afghans. Their rugged terrain has
scattered them as remnants of migratory groups or armies that
moved across inner Asia seeking security or conquest. As a result, every major Asian people has left its mark; among the
eighteen Afghan languages are living descendants of four great
linguistic familes: the Indo-European, Sinic, Semitic, and Dra-
vidian. Afghanistan's demography is a complex mosaic of peoples, locked in a perennial struggle for land, water, and independence.

In recent centuries the Pushtuns have dominated the struggle
for the country's scarce resources. Organized by tribe, these
people speak Pushtu, an offshoot of the Persian language family. Pushtuns claim the eastern and southern sectors of Afghanistan as their ancestral home. Over the past two hundred years
they have extended their power, adding land and subjects until
they have no serious internal rival.

Imposition of Pushtun authority over other groups has produced a measure of uniformity in social and cultural traits,
although certain features of character and behavior had been
shared by most Afghans earlier. Social organization throughout
the country had been based on family or extended kinship units.
For some purposes these basic groups were clustered together
into clan, subtribal, and tribal arrangements, but most aspects of
everyday living concerned only the smallest local units. As the

19

AFGHANISTAN

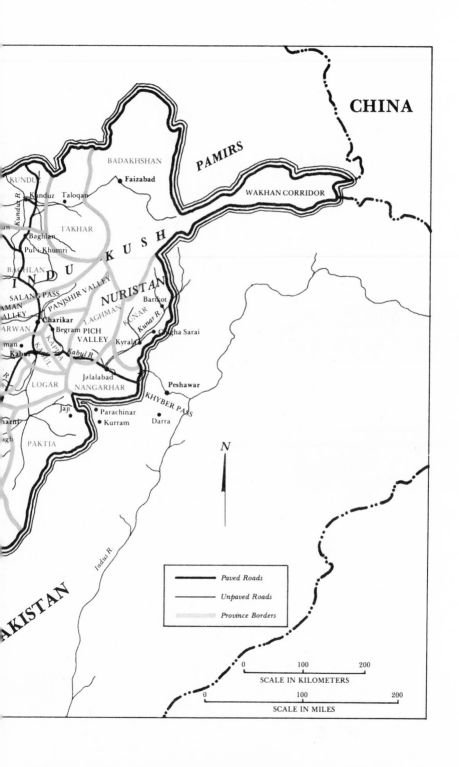

broken landscape often separates people closely related to each other, all Afghan communities stress the autonomy of the primary group as essential to the integrity of their way of life. Reciprocal isolation has usually led to constant friction and conflict over their most valuable resources: land, water, animals. Afghan codes of behavior have therefore come to stress self-reliance, valor, and loyalty to the primary group.

Underlying and connecting the culture of these disparate peoples has been the faith of Islam. Afghan Muslims are identified with the most conservative expressions of the religion. Remote from the intellectual centers of the Islamic world and lacking strong urban institutions, Afghans have developed local variations on Islam's major doctrines, incorporating distinctive beliefs and cults that predate Islam. Often such cults are organized around the veneration of local saints, whose shrines play a major role in focusing the emotional elements of religion. Yet the sharing of a great universal religious tradition has been the strongest force in the society. It is estimated that 80 percent of Afghans belong to the Sunni branch of Islam; the rest, mostly in the more remote parts of the country, are Shias. Despite the near universality of Islam (there are a few thousand Hindus and Sikhs in the towns), religious values have had strikingly little to do with the evolution of a national political system. Common political action based on religion has been obvious only when Afghans have rallied to expel foreign invaders as infidels.

Poverty is almost as widely shared as Islam in Afghanistan. Except for a small number of wealthy traders, nomadic tribal leaders (khans), and the royal family and its retainers, few Afghans have lived far from the basic level of subsistence. Throughout the country their diet consists of coarse bread, tea, and dairy products, supplemented by fruits and vegetables in season and an occasional serving of mutton or chicken. Though food is never plentiful, the Afghan diet during good crop years appears to be sufficient to support a vigorous population, but the precariousness of the food supply is obvious from the drastic and continuing erosion of the soil and the creeping desertization of its landscape.

22

The poverty of most Afghan farmers and herders has imposed an elemental quality on their culture. Values are oriented toward social survival. Loyalty to the primary group ultimately takes precedence over self-assertion, despite the great importance given to personal independence. The conflict between these competing values is a major feature of Afghan life, but in-group loyalty has necessarily played the paramount role in the shaping of attitudes toward fellow Afghans and outsiders.

The dominant Pushtuns have spread through all sectors of the country, although they still are concentrated in the mountainous regions of the east and the south. Despite their political power, the majority of Pushtuns retain a culture based on their sparsely endowed homeland. The origins of these people remain a mystery. Some historians claim that they inhabited the hills between Afghanistan and the Indus River as early as the time of Alexander the Great. Their own lore makes them one of the lost tribes of Israel. It is certain that they were in their traditional region when they were converted to Islam between the eighth and tenth centuries.

Most Pushtuns are farmers, but many mix agriculture with herding. Perhaps as many as one million of them are entirely nomadic. Nearly all are tribally organized. Control over mountain valleys, water rights, and grazing land has formed the essence of Pushtun politics, both among themselves and in their relations with others.

In addition to the basic requirements of Islam, Pushtuns observe the code of *Pushtunwali*. It is simple but demanding. Group survival is its primary imperative. It demands vengeance against injury or insult to one's kin, chivalry and hospitality toward the helpless and unarmed strangers, bravery in battle, and openness and integrity in individual behavior. Much honor is given Pushtuns who can successfully arbitrate the feuds that are endemic among them. Fines and blood money are devices frequently used to limit violence between rival families. Pushtunwali is a code that limits anarchy among a fractious but vital people. It has influenced other groups within the country who must deal with similar environmental and social realities.

23

Pushtun man, Samangan

24

Tajiks, the second largest ethnic community in Afghanistan, live in settled communities, usually as farmers or townspeople. Most are scattered in the eastern and northeastern parts of the country, both north and south of the Hindu Kush. Their language, Dari or Afghan Persian, and Pushtu are the national languages. Their tongue indicates that they and the Iranians share a common origin. As sedentary villagers, the Tajiks have been Afghanistan's most productive farmers.

Turkish people dominate the extreme northern plains adjacent to the Amu Darya (Oxus) River. The most numerous are the Uzbeks. Like the Pushtuns, they practice a mixture of farming and herding. Their most famous products are the fur of the lamb fetus, karakul (Persian lamb), and tribal rugs, usually tied by the women. Male Uzbeks are great horsemen and have developed *buzkashi*, a rugged variation of polo in which teams of horsemen vie in placing the corpse of a goat or a calf behind the other's goal, into the national sport. Many Afghan Uzbeks are relatively recent migrants from the Soviet Union, having fled the Bolshevik conquest of their homeland. Less numerous are the Turkomans, who live in the far northwestern corner of the country. Their largely nomadic economy is similar to that of the Uzbeks; Turkoman women are also famous for their carpets.

The mountainous central region of the country is inhabited by the Hazaras. Stocky in build and Mongoloid in appearance, they have suffered much from the rigors of their climate and the intrusions of their neighbors. They were often enslaved for failure to pay tribute to Pushtun or Uzbek chiefs. Most Hazaras speak a variant of Persian and all but a few are members of the Shia branch of Islam.

Afghanistan has several smaller minority communities, some of which are important by virtue of their strategic locations or unique functions. The Nuristanis control the extremely rugged region north of Jalalabad, immediately adjacent to Pakistan. Spread over a vast desert region that extends from Pakistan across southern Afghanistan to southeastern Iran, the Baluch nomads remain largely a law unto themselves.

All of these peoples live in an exceptionally difficult land-

A *buzkashi* game near Kabul

scape. Most of the countryside is either mountainous or desert. Only some 6 percent of the land is cultivable.[1] The sparseness of rainfall (ten inches or less per year, on the average) and sharp seasonal changes put severe limitations on farming and stock raising. Winters are bitterly cold in nearly all parts of the country; the summers are dry, dusty, and extremely hot. In January and February snow accumulates on most of the mountains and the higher plains. The spring rains last into May. There is almost no precipitation the rest of the year.

The idea of Afghanistan as a remote place is spawned by Western geography. Until modern sea trade took the place of

Hazara women and children, Hazarajat

the storied routes across inner Asia, it was at the hub of world commerce. Even now it is far from being isolated. It is hemmed in by boundaries imposed by European empires. To the north lies Soviet Central Asia, beyond Afghanistan's only natural boundary, the Amu Darya River. To the west is Iran, separated by a British-imposed border that meanders from north to south through desolate country until it intersects with the Pakistani boundary south of the swamps of Sistan. The extremely long border with Pakistan bisects the stony deserts of Baluchistan and then wanders irregularly northeastward through the hilly tribal area that the British never managed to pacify while they were building their Indian empire. The Pakistani border ends in the far northeast, where some fifty miles of boundary is shared with

27

China. This short boundary marks the end of the Wakhan Corridor, which Marco Polo aptly called the "roof of the world." In every direction these borders arbitrarily split the homelands of nomadic peoples, partitioning them between neighboring countries. Instead of suffering from isolation, Afghanistan has found its foreign relations gravely complicated by the fact that it has shared divided peoples with other countries on all sides.

Afghanistan's mountains are exceptionally jagged and stark. Near the Pamirs several peaks reach more than 20,000 feet. Except for a limited area on the eastern side of the country, the mountains are virtually treeless, the result of thousands of years of grazing by sheep and goats and of human exploitation.

Afghanistan's major rivers rise from its central mountain core. They run at full spate in the early spring, as the winter snows melt and the brief rainy season begins. Only one of these river systems, the Kabul, which joins the Indus in northwest Pakistan, flows all the way to the ocean. The Kabul River drains several rich valleys in eastern Afghanistan. From the northern slope of the Hindu Kush the Kunduz River flows north to join the Amu Darya. It waters the plain that the Greeks named Bactria, one of the richest agricultural regions of the country. The most important west-flowing river is the Hari Rud, which created the Herat Valley, established as a prosperous farming region in early antiquity. The Helmand, the largest exclusively Afghan river, takes a long southwesterly course past Kandahar and struggles through the Dasht-i-Margo desert to debouch finally into the salty bogs of Sistan, not far from the Iranian border.

These rivers and their many tributaries provide the basis for settled life throughout the country. The great majority of the population subsists as farmers by diverting the water from the streams onto plots painfully leveled in order to make use of almost every bit of the thin soil that has accumulated in the narrow, winding valleys. The runoff of Afghan rivers is often so thoroughly absorbed by irrigation that little or no flow remains in the stream beds where valleys open out onto the lower plains. Thus the farther one travels away from the mountains in the southern, western, and northern regions of Afghanistan, the

Nomad and daughter, Jalalabad

fewer settled farming communities one is likely to encounter.
Nomads dominate these dry, flat peripheral areas.

Afghanistan's largest and most persistent cities are located
where the largest of the rivers pass out of the mountains into
wide valleys or plains. Kabul, at about 6,000 feet, is favored by a
network of fertile valleys. The city is also strategically placed as
the hub of the trade that has passed between India and the great
Asian roads that crossed Afghanistan north of the Hindu Kush.
Its location also provided some control over the difficult Khyber
Pass region, between Afghanistan and the north Indian plains.

Each of the other major cities dominates a quadrant of the
country. In the southeast, Kandahar commands routes passing
through the southern deserts to connect with passes that bring
the traveler into Baluchistan or the lower Indus basin. To the far

west, Herat has remained the place where travelers across northern Afghanistan can connect with the only practicable routes around the mountains toward Kandahar and India. Newer cities are Kunduz, which has grown rapidly since malaria was brought under control in the 1950s, and Mazar-i-Sharif, successor to Balkh, the ancient caravan center known as the "Mother of Cities."

Afghanistan's smaller cities are typically found in upper valleys at points where farming can be concentrated and trade routes may cross. The most important of these towns are Faizabad, in the far northeast; Bamiyan, in the central mountain massif; and Ghazni, on the road between Kabul and Kandahar. Other cities are located at strategic points on the plains at the far edges of the country. Among them are Shibarghan and Maimana, in the far northwest; Farah, in the southwest; and Jalalabad, in the extreme east, near the Khyber Pass.

Afghan farmers raise wheat, cotton, fruits, and vegetables. The most productive land is irrigated, although cereal crops can be irregularly harvested along the slopes of the valleys when rainfall is sufficient. Three-fourths of the population depend on farming for their livelihood; most of the rest practice various forms of nomadism. Many farmers combine cultivation with some form of wandering, often to graze their animals in mountain meadows during the summer. The true nomads, estimated to be as many as 2 million, move from their lowland winter camps upward through the valleys to the mountains in the spring and summer, taking advantage of the brief ripening of grass in the stingy soil as the season progresses. The pattern of nomadic movement is that of a gigantic folk dance, forming a large circle in the winter and then converging into the central mountainous core in the summer.

Relations between farmers and herders are full of tension. Each needs the other, trading crops for animal products. Nomads also serve as traders and often as bankers for farmers in the more remote uplands. Their conflicts center on competition over land.

Afghanistan's meager and eroding agricultural resources support a population estimated to be close to 15 million; there has never been a complete census. The major industrial mineral deposits, most of them only recently discovered and surveyed, have not been exploited. There are world-class deposits of iron, chrome, and copper ores and possibly of uranium.[2] There are also sizable deposits of soft coal. All of these minerals are located in difficult mountain country; their extraction and processing would require heavy investments in roads and construction. Pockets of natural gas have recently been discovered. Surveys suggest there may be exploitable deposits of oil and gas in the northern plains and perhaps in the western and southern deserts. The rivers could provide enough hydroelectric power to support modest industrial development. Small beginnings were made in the development of these resources in the 1950s and 1960s.

The most dramatic progress was made in tying the country together with all-season roads, airline connections, and telecommunications facilities. The largest cities are now served by a system of paved roads that loops from the Soviet border in the far northwest through Herat and Kandahar to Kabul and then north through the Salang Pass in the Hindu Kush to Kunduz and on through Mazar-i-Sharif to the Amu Darya, at a spot opposite the town of Termez, in the Uzbek S.S.R. Paved roads connect this system to Iran and to Pakistan.

Commercial airlines link all sectors of the country, including many of the smaller provincial capitals. The major military air bases are at Shindand, a short distance south of Herat, and at Begram, north of Kabul. Both the Kabul and the Kandahar airports are equipped for international air service and can operate as large military bases. A microwave telephone system installed in the 1960s brought nearly all subprovincial offices into direct communication with the capital.

These recent developments have transformed the prospects for physical unification of the country. Travel from Herat to Kabul took six weeks in 1900; most Afghans can now reach any but the most remote parts of their country within one or two days. Such beginnings of modernization left their country espe-

Farmer, Bamiyan

cially vulnerable to sudden internal tumults and to foreign intervention. The new roads have not yet linked Afghans into a tightly unified society, but they have enabled foreign armored divisions to sweep across the plains and deserts within a few days.

2

The Rise and Fall of
the Afghan Monarchy

Afghanistan's emergence as a nation was the product of royal leadership. The monarchy was founded on the basis of a tribal confederation that was intended to prevent anarchy and foreign invasions. The kings gave a central focus to the political system first by acting as leaders among equals with the tribal khans, later by strengthening central power at the expense of the tribes and other autonomous groups throughout the country.

In the nineteenth century, as the British and Russian imperial powers pressed on Afghanistan, the role of the kings became more complex. It required a delicate balancing of external diplomacy and internal repression while modern organization and technology were introduced. In the twentieth century the monarchy struggled to maintain this precarious balance. By the early 1970s the task had become so complicated that the royal system broke down despite creative and innovative efforts to extend and modify its structure. The last king, Zahir Shah, ruled until 1973.[1] For the next five years his cousin and brother-in-law, Muhammad Daoud, governed as a royal president. He and his republic did not survive to solve the problems they inherited. The Marxists who seized power in 1978 stepped into a vacuum created by the ultimate failure of the monarchy to cope with the multiplying problems of change, unity, and national independence.

The peoples of the region that would become Afghanistan had first been unified in 1747, in a tribal confederation led by

Ahmad Shah Durrani (1747–73). The shah, the talented leader of a relatively minor Pushtun tribe, was accepted because his ability to interfere with the major khans was limited. His confederacy prospered through the use of plunder as a tactic for political unity. Throughout the winters of the 1750s and 1760s his composite tribal armies ranged over the north Indian plains, plundering whatever they could carry off to share upon their return. Such successes could ensure only a tenuous unity, and when Ahmad Shah's son and grandsons proved incapable of continuing the profitable raids, the armies of the confederation disintegrated and the many claimants for his throne fell to fighting among themselves. Unity was not restored even in the most superficial sense until Dost Muhammad (1826–39, 1843–63), another leader of genius, emerged in the 1830s to subdue his rivals. His success in uniting the country politically furnished part of the reason for Britain's intervention in 1839. Three years of war against the Pushtun tribes brought disaster to the British and established Dost Muhammad more firmly on his throne. By the end of his reign he had reunited Afghanistan into a single political unit.

Its role as a buffer state between the British and the Russians became crucial during the reign of Dost Muhammad. Afghan rulers were forced to develop policies that would ensure effective control over internal politics while fending off threats from those powerful empires. These challenges led to a dual policy of diplomatic agility and internal consolidation. The first steps began with Amir Ali (1863–79), who started the modern organization of the royal staff and hired foreign educators and military advisers. Substantial progress toward achievement of central control came through the leadership of Abdur Rahman (1880–1901), who was able to suppress all overt opposition. In a series of campaigns in the 1890s he subdued the independent Uzbek khans of the north, the Hazaras of the central mountains, and the Kafirs (Nuristanis) of the far northeast. With British assistance he suppressed all internal opposition. The British supplied the money to build a standing army that gave Abdur Rahman dominance over all regional groups in the country. The cost of this subsidy was his acceptance of British control over foreign affairs. The formula ensured him of protection against the Russians, who were consolidating their conquest of Central Asia during his reign.

The Iron Amir, as Abdur Rahman was known, recognized that his control over the country could never be secure unless he could keep British influence at arm's length. He consistently resisted British requests to station diplomats and military detachments within his country. For the same reason he rejected offers to extend the railway system of British India into his kingdom and offers of aid in the development of the Afghan economy. Abdur Rahman appreciated the importance of modern technology and of administrative techniques that would consolidate his control, but he limited foreign influence by using a small number of foreign advisers as personal employees. Actual technical innovations were limited to the establishment of armament factories capable of producing hand weapons, crude artillery pieces, and ammunition.

Unity under Abdur Rahman was established primarily through political measures. Hostages were taken from subdued tribes and forced to live at the royal court. Islamic religious leaders were required to declare their loyalty to the throne and to agree that Abdur Rahman had religious sanction to impose his rule. Particularly stubborn Pushtuns were forced to migrate to regions that were largely uninhabited or settled by groups hostile to the government. Such migrants were bribed by grants of land that ensured royal control over their claims.

Abdur Rahman's tactics brought about the consolidation of central power for the first time. His system was continued by his son, Habibullah (1901–19). During Habibullah's reign the pace of modernization increased slightly. Electric power and the automobile were introduced and all-weather roads were built. The ruling elite began to develop a taste for manufactured products imported from British India. Some members of the court began to entertain modern non-Islamic social and political ideas. Essentially, however, Habibullah ruled as his father had done, with slightly less ferocity.

Royal policy changed drastically with the accession of Amanullah (1919–29), who took the title of shah or king. Fascinated by nearly all aspects of Western life, he embarked on a new foreign policy and initiated an ambitious series of political, social, and cultural reforms. Early in his reign Amanullah declared war on the British, who were then preoccupied with the explosion of Indian nationalism at the end of World War I. Six weeks of fighting, waged mostly by Pushtun tribes, led to a treaty in which the British recognized Afghanistan's full independence. At the same time he maneuvered for a new relationship with Russia, now coming under the control of the Bolsheviks. Hailing Lenin's claim that the Soviets were opposed to all forms of European imperialism, Amanullah rushed into a temporary alliance with them. It yielded a small amount of military aid, including the beginnings of an air force. Later, when the Soviets ran into serious opposition from the Turkish people of Central Asia, he attempted to intervene, aligning himself with Enver Pasha and other Turkish leaders who were attempting to keep the Bolsheviks out of the region. When the Turks failed, Amanullah shifted back to a policy of friendship with Moscow. These foreign-policy initiatives added greatly to Afghanistan's independence in international and particularly inter-Asian affairs at a time when few Islamic countries were free of European control. His policies were seen as achieving a new status for Islam.

In internal matters Amanullah was committed to ambitious change. His policies imitated those of the Western powers whose interference in the country he was so determined to prevent. He overhauled government administration and established a Western form of ministerial cabinet. Afghanistan's first constitution, patterned after continental European models, established a parliament with quasi-legislative authority. A modern educational system structured on a European curriculum was introduced, first in Kabul and later in other cities. Muslim teachers were imported from India, Turkey, and Egypt for the first time. By the mid-1920s a number of English, French, German, and Italian instructors were employed and their languages were taught. Plans were drawn up for a national system of education. Specialized schools of nursing and other vocational studies were founded. These moves incorporated the dramatic innovation of permitting, in some cases even requiring, women to play public roles in society. The women of the royal family appeared unveiled in public and the families of the aristocracy felt strong pressure to send their daughters to school. Amanullah also attempted to modernize Kabul through the construction of public buildings.

Amanullah's commitment to change increased as his reign advanced. In 1928 he and Queen Soraya completed a royal tour of Europe, including the Soviet Union. On their return he proclaimed a series of reforms that would have undercut the autonomy of the tribes and the influence of the mullahs. As these ambitious plans were not accompanied by measures to strengthen the government's control, tribal and religious leaders had little difficulty in fomenting a successful revolt. When Kabul came under siege by tribal armies, Amanullah abdicated and fled the country.

The collapse of Amanullah's government provided an object lesson on the dangers of trying to impose abrupt and profound changes on a people unprepared for them. His reforms demonstrated the need for skilled economic planning and corps of trained administrators. The reaction to his reforms showed the perils of sudden changes in the roles of women and Islam in Afghan life. The resulting collapse of the central government was the first such crisis the country had faced since Abdur Rahman consolidated it in the nineteenth century. For nine months Kabul was governed by Bacha Saquo, a peasant rebel; much of the rest of the country lapsed into anarchy.

Out of this chaos came a cautious restoration by a collateral branch of Amanullah's family, the Musahibans. The founder of the new dynasty was Nadir Khan, who took the title of shah in 1929. Formerly a general under Amanullah, Nadir had retired to France in the mid-1920s after policy disagreements with the shah. He seized the throne with the support of the British, who feared tribal uprisings on their Indian border, and with the additional help of a Pushtun tribal confederation. The restoration alienated the Soviet Union, which had favored Amanullah's progressive goals and hostility toward the British. The Musahibans were not to resume friendly relations with the Soviet Union until after Stalin's death.

To build its power base the new royal government moved to conciliate the tribes. The king and his four brothers operated as the political hub of a patronage network that emphasized personal ties with the khans and other regional leaders, in the traditional fashion. This policy required the relaxation of central control in some crucial areas of authority. Some of the tribes that had brought the Musahibans to power were excused from taxation and military conscription. With British financial help and the aid of German advisers, however, the royal brothers succeeded in rebuilding the central security forces. By the late 1930s the regime's control over all areas of the country was unchallenged. In the course of reestablishing royal power, the government resorted to repressive measures that undermined its support among the elite. The narrowness of its base of support among the well off and the well educated proved later to be a serious liability.

The new government was extremely cautious on social and cultural matters. The school system, which had collapsed during the civil war, was only partially restored; schooling was no longer offered to women, who were forced back under the veil. The roles of foreign educational advisers were restricted, although more technical experts were employed for economic projects. Innovation, in fact, was channeled almost exclusively toward economic change. A central bank was established and many private corporations were licensed to develop foreign trade, particularly in hides, wool, carpets, and food products. These new firms also made possible the importation of foreign goods, especially tea and sugar from India and manufactured items from Europe. The revenue gained by this considerably expanded commercial activity was intended to build up the military and internal security forces.

World War II presented a severe challenge to the government. Both the British and the Soviets insisted on the internment of German and Italian advisers. Throughout the war the Kabul government managed to maintain a precarious independence tied to neutrality, but this posture did little to improve its relations with the Soviets.

Modernization and the Monarchy

The end of the war brought changes in Asia that swept Afghanistan into a new international era. European imperialism receded with the departure of the British from India and the creation of Muslim Pakistan on its eastern border. Moreover, the war had transformed the Soviet Union from a huge nation obsessed with defending its revolution into an aggressive superpower. Stimulated by these circumstances and by the pressures for political, social, and economic change being felt by Third World nations, the Afghan government committed itself to unprecedented innovations. A generation had passed since Amanullah had sent a small group of students to Europe for advanced education. The few hundred Western-educated Afghans now clamored for reforms. They wanted greater career opportunities for themselves and more education for their children. To achieve its new development goals, the royal government had to rely on the skills of these educated people, whose cooperation it could win only by sharing political power with them. Such a course would require the regime to relax its authoritarian methods and revise the patronage system, dominated by the royal family. The struggle to maintain power while relaxing authority was to dominate the political scene for a quarter of a century, until the monarchy lost control over the process.

The need for foreign aid to develop the country economically dictated an overhaul of Afghanistan's diplomatic strategies. Britain was gone from India, but the pressure from the USSR was potentially greater than ever. The task of establishing a balance between great powers had become much more difficult. The new formula called for the government to equalize foreign influence by attracting development assistance from a whole spectrum of nations throughout the world. Kabul was to become a diplomatic crossroads. Such a strategy was extraordinary for a country whose exposure to the modern international community had been limited and which had almost universally been seen as remote and unimportant.

Even more remarkable was the degree of success that was achieved. By the 1970s, more than twenty nations operated bilateral aid programs in the country. The donors included the United States, all Western European countries, most of the Eastern European communist bloc, the larger or wealthier Muslim nations, and the principal Asian states.

American-Afghan relations had been fully established in 1943. Shortly after World War II the Kabul government turned to the United States for the diplomatic support it could no longer expect from Great Britain. In the late 1940s the United States was also the most promising source of economic aid. Thus was launched an increasingly intimate relationship that eventually led the United States to have considerable impact on Afghan efforts in agriculture, education, transportation, and economic planning. At no time, however, did the United States take over the British role of powerful protector, and after 1955 the Soviets gained increasing influence.

Outside assistance enabled the Kabul government to strengthen its military and internal security forces to the point where central control could not be challenged while fundamental social and economic changes were being introduced. Amanullah's disaster was to be avoided. The United States was the first major power approached for military assistance. The request was turned down on the grounds that an increase in Afghan military capacity would be a dangerous provocation to the USSR. Such military support also would have conflicted with American plans to build up Pakistan's military forces. A serious diplomatic impasse had developed with Pakistan over the status of the Pushtun people living on the Pakistani side of the border. This American decision compelled the Afghan government to turn to the Soviet Union for the military assistance it sought. From this point onward, Soviet intervention in the political system was ensured. The monarchy had to combine conciliation with reliance on the Soviet Union in its efforts to control and modernize the country. Beginning in 1954 the Kremlin was to supply virtually all equipment and training for the Afghan army and air force. The Afghan officer corps typically received several years of military training and political exposure in the Soviet Union.[2]

The move toward the Soviet Union was engineered by Prince Muhammad Daoud, who assumed the office of prime minister in 1953. Daoud was to run the country as a strongman on behalf of the king, his cousin Zahir, for the next ten years. Daoud's regime continued the generally oppressive style of rule adopted by his uncles in the 1930s. Under Daoud blueprints for national development were drawn up. He concentrated on nation building in the form of physical projects, the strengthening of government agencies, and the establishment of an ambitious set of educational programs. These efforts were intended to bring about rapid modernization. Yet there were political contradictions. His no-nonsense approach combined such initiatives as the reemergence of women into public life with the prohibition of virtually all political activity by the growing middle class. Political rights were deferred while Daoud focused on building the foundations for improvements in living conditions.

Economically this first Daoud era was marked by considerable success. A basis was laid for a modern transportation system; roads were paved, air connections established, and telecommunications opened. Agriculture and education were greatly expanded. Large numbers of Afghans were trained inside and outside the country to staff teaching institutions and the burgeoning development agencies of the government. In almost all areas other than the military, the influence of Western nations, especially the United States, was prominent. Soviet aid was also important in economic projects, especially road, power, and petroleum development. Daoud therefore achieved a balance in sources of aid which appeared to offset the Soviet military role.[3]

In only one political area did Daoud welcome popular participation: the issue of Pushtunistan. Friction arose over the status of the Pushtun people living in Pakistan. The internationally recognized boundary was the result of an understanding reached between the British government of India and Abdur Rahman in 1893. That agreement had also set up a method of pacifying the turbulent Pushtun people who lived in the mountains between Afghanistan and the Indus River. The Afghan government, maintaining that the rights of the Pushtuns to reject Pakistani nationality had not been recognized when the British partitioned India in 1947, now rejected the 1893 line (the Durand Line) as the Afghan-Pakistani boundary. That line, they claimed, marked off the areas in which the British and Afghan governments were responsible for controlling tribal peoples.[4] There was genuine sentiment among Afghans, especially among the Pushtuns, in favor of maintaining close political ties with Pushtun tribesmen in Pakistan. Out of this conflict arose the claim that the Pushtuns of Pakistan should have the option of creating their own nation, to be carved out of Pakistan west of the Indus River. Presumably this new nation would be loosely affiliated with Afghanistan, which after all was a nation governed by Pushtuns. Afghanistan's demand for autonomy for the Pushtuns of Pakistan was tantamount to claiming control over Pushtunistan, since the unification of the Pushtuns would come under the control of the Kabul government. This disagreement festered throughout Daoud's prime ministership and led to several crises when Pakistan closed its borders to trade vital to Afghanistan. Daoud kept the issue alive at least partly to generate Pushtun support while permitting no expressions of opinion on most other subjects. This policy gave Zahir Shah a pretext to dismiss his cousin and introduce an experiment in liberal reform in 1963.[5]

Constitutional Liberalism, 1963–73

Daoud's policy of economic development with political repression had produced great change and ferment, particularly among the rapidly growing educated middle class. His removal was popular, as it provided an opportunity for this new class to share power with the royal family. By this time some Afghans had achieved eminence in scholarship, the liberal professions, and the technocratic areas of government. Zahir Shah's call for a popularly elected parliament that would share power with a cabinet answerable to him was greeted with enthusiasm. In 1964 a new constitution was ratified by a *loya jirgah*, a formal gathering of the traditional religious and political leaders of all communities. The constitution established the basis for popular government and equal civil rights for men and women. The following year a national election was held. The limited criticism of the results suggests there was little rigging. The promise of this new era of open competition among groups and ideas was most evident in the sudden freedom of the intellectuals and professionals to associate openly with each other and with foreigners. This freedom of expression and association was to continue until Daoud returned to power in 1973.[6]

The promise of the new era was blighted by the dangers posed by volatile political groups. Riots broke out in October 1965, when several thousand students and political activists attempted to prevent the parliament's ratification of the cabinet nominated by the king's interim government. The ensuing bloodshed was limited, but the government was shocked into a realization of the public turbulence made possible by the new freedoms.[7] It became cautious. The liberal reforms were halfheartedly implemented and were allowed to stagnate. The supreme court that was to have enforced laws and personal rights independently of the executive was never allowed to function. Political parties that could have disciplined members of parliament and political activists continued to be illegal. Private newspapers were permitted, but considerable pressure was applied to keep them in line, and some of the more outspoken were suppressed. As a result of these limitations, the liberal experiment was too weak to survive. While the educated class benefited from expansion of opportunity and political expression, it did not identify itself with the fate of the reforms. It was given too little responsibility to develop self-discipline and too little power to be totally committed. The result was a splintering of political behavior and a growing cynicism toward government in general. Opportunism and corruption, amply fed by the possibilities for enrichment from the many streams of foreign assistance, demoralized the country's leadership.[8]

Disillusionment was aggravated by economic problems. Once the major roads were built and dams and irrigation facilities constructed, economic progress depended on growing skills in managing the economy as a whole. The activities of several specialized ministries and agencies had to be coordinated. The government's ability to harness resources for productive investment required realistic policies of taxation, credit controls, and foreign trade. Land development, agricultural innovation, and the operation of new industries required organizational and technical expertise. In short, development was moving from the construction of physical facilities to their operation. The dual challenge of managing the growth of the economy and broadening the political system proved to be more than the government and the new educated class could handle. Economic conditions were further aggravated by the falling off of interest by foreign donors. By the early 1970s a large share of the incoming aid was offset by debt payments owed on previous loans.[9] Before the liberal government was able to benefit from help that might have come from newly enriched Muslim OPEC nations, the liberal experiment was dead.

Despite its limitations, the liberal era left a permanent mark. The middle class had expanded from a few hundred to nearly 100,000.[10] Kabul truly became a cosmopolitan center of trade, diplomacy, and international intrigue. Its achievements ensured that whatever the direction of the country's politics in the future, it could not be reversed.

The Afghan Republic: An Epilogue to the Monarchy

Muhammad Daoud's return to power by a nearly bloodless coup brought the false promise of a new era. Offering the rhetoric of republican populism, his regime ultimately served as a transition from monarchy to a Marxist dictatorship. Returning to power in his late sixties, Daoud proceeded to create a government that mixed the political repression of his previous regime with the confusion over goals and strategy that marked Zahir Shah's last years. The focus of a personality cult from the moment he seized power on July 17, 1973, Daoud ruled more as king than as a suddenly elevated commoner. Ironically, his control over the government was never certain enough to permit him to act with confidence as either king or president. In the end he found himself without the support of the elite, either traditional or modern, or of his Marxist partners, or of his Soviet allies. His last regime brought the definitive end of the Afghan monarchy.

The circumstances of his return to power sharply limited Daoud's ability to rule as dynamically as he had done as prime minister from 1953 to 1963. He owed his return to the Parcham wing of the Marxist People's Democratic Party of Afghanistan (PDPA), which had planned and carried out the coup by infiltrating crucial army and air force units. Parcham's Marxist leaders chose to ally themselves with him apparently in the belief that he could win popular acceptance and would be receptive to their political program. In plotting his return to power, Daoud committed himself to the social program and pro-Soviet posture of the Marxists.[11]

Within months of his return to power, Daoud began to maneuver for total control of the government. This attempt forced him to divert much of his energy to expelling Marxists from the cabinet and the governing revolutionary council. By 1976, when he had finally consolidated his position, he had lost much time and political capital.

Daoud's struggle to gain control manifested itself in a wide swing to the right in overall policy. Originally his government's rhetoric called for mass support of the republic's revolutionary program of social and political reforms and reinvigorated economic development. The Soviet Union rushed to support the government with increased military aid and a spurt of development proposals, especially in petroleum exploration, mining surveys, road construction, agricultural development, and technical education. Parcham leaders were installed in the ministries of Agriculture, Education, Communications, and Frontier

Affairs. Ambitious reforms were designed for education and land redistribution. Insurance and banking were nationalized. Major reforms were also introduced in agricultural taxation, commercial and criminal law, the civil service, and police organization. The republic not only projected a leftist image; it also reimposed authoritarian controls on the population. Restrictions were placed on political activity and contacts with the many foreigners in Kabul. Tentative moves toward self-government at the university were blocked by rigid bureaucratic controls. Security forces, particularly the police, were reorganized and strengthened by the inducement of higher pay and other incentives. At least two countercoups were crushed and a number of alleged plotters executed with much publicity.[12]

In 1975 Daoud began to purge the Parcham leaders, but he retained the general thrust of their programs. He attempted to replace them with political retainers close to him and moderate or nonpartisan officials from the previous liberal cabinets. These adjustments were accompanied by the promulgation in early 1977 of yet another constitution, Afghanistan's fourth. Drafted with some care as a liberal document, with provisions guaranteeing equal rights for men and women and restricting Islam to a passive role, the constitution attempted to make Daoud's political power total through a strong presidency and a weak legislature. By authorizing a one-party structure, the constitution was tailored to promote a monolithic popular party to support Daoud, whom it named as president. Initial elections were scheduled for November 1979.[13] Daoud and his closest advisers concentrated so single-mindedly on the political problems of consolidating power that economic and social issues were left unattended or in confusion. The popular support given Daoud in anticipation of quick and effective reforms and economic improvements waned as political maneuvering consumed his leadership.

By the mid-1970s Afghanistan was facing the growing calamities of partial development. Its exploding secondary school system was graduating nearly 20,000 students per year.[14] Fewer than half of those graduates could find places in the university

47

or postsecondary professional schools. There were virtually no jobs for the educated except possibly in teaching. Unemployment of the educated was compounded by steep inflation. Both unemployment and inflation were aggravated by an accelerating tide of migration from countryside to city, especially to Kabul, where the population was pressing close to one million. It was also clear that the country was imperiled by its failure to expand the production of food for either subsistence or export earnings. Obsessed by its political problems, the regime was being undercut by a growing inability to cope with popular needs.

Daoud's determination to gain total control cost him the support of all groups with political influence. Most of the liberals who had served the constitutional monarchy had been purged or shoved aside. Religious conservatives were persecuted. Muhammad Niazi, leader of the fundamentalist Ikwan-i-Musalamin (Islamic Brotherhood), was jailed. Two of his lieutenants, Burhanuddin Rabani and Gulbuddin Hekmatyar, fled to Pakistan, where they set up resistance organizations. The leftists bitterly turned against Daoud once it became clear that he was determined to destroy their influence in the government. Except for a few Marxists who had disguised their affiliation, none occupied an important position by 1977. Daoud's relations with the traditionally important tribal and community leaders throughout the country had also been seriously weakened by the actions of his government. The often arrogant young Marxists assigned to provincial posts frequently provoked confrontations with the khans and other rural notables. In the process, the republican government became identified with what were viewed as disruptive, radical attempts to overturn the structure of rural society. Particularly resented were the introduction of a mild degree of land reform, a policy of tenant protection, controls over rural credit, and increased agricultural taxes that fell most heavily on the largest landholders.

An old man, Daoud appeared no longer to be capable of solving political and economic problems simultaneously. Instead, he appeared increasingly to be groping for short-term solutions and relying on security measures to keep himself in power. His National Revolutionary Party, established in connection with the constitution of 1977, was seen as a personal instrument to maintain him in power. Recruitment into the party was seen not as evidence of personal commitment or support, but rather as a means of securing jobs and other favors.

The growing political vacuum around Daoud was accompanied by a change in foreign policy. Simultaneously with his purge of the Parchamists, Daoud moved to disengage his government from the Soviet embrace. One vehicle for close Afghan-Soviet relations had been revival of the Pushtunistan issue. For the first two years of the republic, Kabul escalated its claims against Pakistan, alleging mistreatment of the Pushtun population. Responding to pressure from other Muslim nations, Daoud began to defuse the issue in 1975 and turned to personal diplomacy to strengthen his relations with the Muslim bloc. Reciprocal state visits by Prime Minister Zulfikar Ali Bhutto of Pakistan and Daoud in 1975 dampened the irritating aspects of the dispute as the two leaders concentrated on plans to expand trade and even to develop a project that could ultimately give Afghanistan transit rights through Pakistani Baluchistan to the port of Gwadar, on the Arabian Sea.

The rapprochement with Pakistan was followed by a concerted effort to strengthen relations with other Muslim nations. The shah of Iran had earlier shown his concern over Soviet and Marxist influence in Kabul by offering to make economic aid available in unprecedented amounts. In 1974 Iran announced the commitment of credits totaling $2 billion.[15] The core of this assistance would be the construction of a 900-mile railroad linking the major iron deposits at Hajigak with Iran, and thus connecting Kabul, Kandahar, and Herat with the outside world. The Iranian credits also were to support projects in agriculture, worker training, and industry. The new era of amity between Iran and Afghanistan had been heralded by Daoud's acceptance of an agreement to share the waters of the lower Helmand River basin, which is divided by their joint border. This agreement and Iranian economic help were celebrated by Daoud's state visit to Iran in 1976.

Relations with other Persian Gulf states were also quickly strengthened through personal diplomacy. Kuwait, Iraq, and Saudi Arabia made commitments to provide aid—commitments that amounted to a radical shift in the sources of assistance, as indicated in Tables 1 and 2. Daoud's campaign to improve Afghanistan's relations with Islamic leaders culminated in a visit to Cairo early in 1978.

These moves toward the Muslim nations appear to have reflected Daoud's recognition of the potential strength of the Muslim states if they acted as a united community. The benefits included political as well as economic support. These moves unquestionably gave Afghanistan leverage to operate independently of Soviet pressure. A further boon was the opportunity to open up trade with the suddenly affluent OPEC nations, especially in Afghan fruit and meat products. Another important source of foreign earnings was the demand for unskilled workers in the rapidly developing Persian Gulf states. By 1977 several hundred thousand Afghan migrants were employed in Iran and smaller numbers were working in the other Gulf nations.

Regional development and the growing sense of Islamic dynamism, which had gained great momentum from the petroleum revolution of the early 1970s, gave Afghanistan the opportunity to realign its foreign relations in a direction away from primary reliance on the USSR. By the late 1960s the United States had already made clear its intention to reduce foreign aid. The American profile in Afghanistan was diminishing, partly because an increasing proportion of American aid was now being channeled through such international agencies as the World Bank, the International Monetary Fund, and the Asian Development Bank. Yet indirect American influence may have worried the Kremlin as it observed the erosion of its own position in Afghanistan. Whatever his motives, Daoud's moves further alienated the Afghan Marxists, and the new direction of his policy certainly gave the Soviet Union cause to reconsider its support.

In the final year of Daoud's republican government, broadened international contacts were offset by a serious decline in

Table 1. Sources of foreign assistance to Afghanistan's development, to 1971 (millions of dollars)

Donor	Amount
USSR	$517.1
U.S.A.	397.6
West Germany	78.2
People's Republic of China	21.1
France	18.5
Czechoslovakia	14.2
United Kingdom	10.9
Other bilateral aid	9.3
United Nations agencies	51.4
Other multilateral aid	16.9

Source: Ministry of Planning, Royal Government of Afghanistan, *Statistical Pocket-Book of Afghanistan* (Kabul, 1971–72), Table 99, p. 163.

Table 2. Anticipated donors for the Daoud republic's seven-year plan, 1976–83 (millions of dollars)

Donor	Amount
Iran	$1,141.6
USSR	570.5
Kuwait	115.2
World Bank	77.9
Czechoslovakia	70.9
Asian Development Bank	70.5
Saudi Arabia	63.5
West Germany	29.1
U.S.A.	22.2
People's Republic of China	20.7
Bulgaria	19.8
United Nations agencies	19.0
France	16.5
Iraq	8.1
India	6.2
Romania	5.0
Japan	3.1
Yugoslavia	2.5
International consortia	131.2

Source: Louis Duprée, "Afghanistan 1977: Does Trade Plus Aid Guarantee Development?," *American Universities Field Staff Reports*, South Asia Series, 21, no. 3 (1977):10.

internal support. After ten years of bickering and rivalry, the Marxist factions found in repression by the government a compelling reason to unite. The Khalq and Parcham factions of the PDPA agreed to set aside their differences and join in a common organization in 1977. This agreement appears to have resulted at least partly from Soviet prodding, and it is possible that leaders of the Communist Party of India acted as mediators. In any event, the two Marxist factions now were in a stronger position to challenge the Daoud regime.

With Daoud's sudden death on April 28, 1978, his republican regime took on the appearance of a curious addendum to Afghanistan's long history of royal rule. More than any other Afghan leader he was responsible for the remarkable acceleration of change over the past quarter century; yet Daoud seems to have been severely crippled by a narrow view of government and a heavy hand in managing the groups and issues that resulted from the changes he initiated. To the end he was most comfortable with the style of the royal autocrat in an era when such a manner of operation was proving impossible. Despite his achievements, at the end he was increasingly relying on toadies at court and in the armed forces and police to maintain control over the country. His era passed virtually without regret.

3

Marxism in Afghanistan

Despite the Marxists' spectacular success in seizing control in April 1978, Afghan Marxism has a short history. Significant Marxist organization began only in 1965. In the years that followed, the party's limited appeal and the bitter factionalism that divided its leaders provided little evidence that Marxists were capable of offering a serious threat to the government. Yet the key role played by the Parcham faction in restoring Daoud to power in 1973 indicated that as the strength of the monarchy declined, the Marxists wielded increasing influence on political events. Marxists were able to rise to power because their opponents were unprepared to deal with the threat that they posed. Their seizure of power was also aided by a growing malaise in political circles which resulted from the government's inability to cope with the problems and opportunities of modernization.

By the 1970s the burgeoning newly educated middle class was increasingly restless and frustrated. Education, often in foreign countries, had prepared many more Afghans to serve in positions of technical and managerial expertise than could be accommodated by the rigid administrative system. The royal government's bureaucracy was staffed in accordance with the traditional court patronage system, slightly modified by a hodgepodge of modern managerial adjustments. The norms of loyalty through blood and traditional attachment clashed with the need for flexibility and efficiency, especially in development administration. Most Afghans with a modern education had been exposed to the intellectual and institutional environments of developed countries. When they returned home (an extremely high percentage of Afghans did return) they found few opportunities that matched either their training or their ambitions. Often their placement in government service appeared to be illogical or arbitrary. It was almost universally believed that one needed connections, either personal or familial, with the royal patronage network to get an attractive job. The resulting resentment was especially dangerous because few career avenues were open to the educated other than government employment. The modern private sector of the economy had experienced little growth. Such new firms as were set up were frequently extensions of trading operations already controlled by established commercial families. Positions in the factories, banks, and trading organizations built and operated by the government required the same access to patronage as government jobs.

The frustrations and bitterness arising from the growing imbalance between educated candidates and suitable jobs were deepened by a growing gap between the standard of living of the few who were amassing wealth and that of the many educated who were not. Fortunes were being made in real estate, import-export operations, and tourism while most of the educated were unemployed or forced to take low-paying jobs.

As Kabul grew, opportunities for speculative investment increased along with urban congestion and crowding. As the pace of city life quickened and prices rose, the lives of people who attempted to lead a middle-class existence became progressively more difficult. For many people, ambition and hope gave way to the conviction that the political system offered little prospect for improvement in their lives. Yet as the school system expanded and the evidence of wealth spread outward from the cities into the countryside, offering glimpses of possible social advancement, an increasing number of young men were drawn into a process of modernization outside of their original circles of family and community. While this process was not unique to Afghanistan, the unpreparedness of its institutions to cope with it was becoming chronic by the late 1960s. For example, when Kabul University was resettled on its modern campus in 1962, it enrolled some 3,000 students and was able to admit all of the graduating secondary school students in the country. By 1966 the number of secondary school graduates had increased so greatly that the university had to introduce entrance examinations, and many young men suddenly found themselves excluded. The situation rapidly became worse when the secondary school system was expanded between 1965 and 1973. Education, which appeared to be the path toward unlimited opportunity, was now a trap for many members of the most volatile segment of the population. Their frustration provided fertile ground for the emergence of antigovernment movements on both the Marxist left and the Islamic right.

Tensions generated by the growing imbalance between opportunity and ambition were increased by the diversity of foreign influences operating on the educational system. These influences acted to complicate absorption of modern ideas and techniques. Virtually every major sector of the economy, government, and education came to be identified with a specific foreign assistance program. For instance, Kabul University's engineering, agriculture, and education faculties were identified with American aid programs; its medicine and law faculties were aided by the French; its natural science and economics faculties were assisted by German programs; its polytechnic faculty was assisted by the Soviets; its Islamic law faculty received Egyptian aid. This fragmentation of the country's major educational institution, which required the use of competing foreign languages as the media for instruction (and simultaneous translation into the mother tongues of students not conversant with English, French, German, and the rest), suggests the difficulty of developing coherent programs to modernize the country. Such fragmentation was mirrored in government organization: the Ministry of Commerce was identified with American aid; the Ministry of Mines and Industries was influenced primarily by Europe and the USSR; and the ministries of Health and Justice were greatly influenced by their French affiliations. Some ministries, notably the Ministry of Planning and to a lesser extent the Ministry of Education, were divided internally on the basis of foreign affiliations and training. Similar divisions affected the specialized agencies. Ariana, the national airline, was supported by Pan American Airways, and the Afghan Construction Unit, responsible for the modern highways, was also closely tied to American aid; telecommunications were developed under West German influence and the petroleum industry was totally affiliated with the Soviets. Various regional agricultural development programs were supported exclusively by American, Soviet, Chinese, and United Nations assistance agencies.

All such foreign affiliations were tied to separate arrangements for the training, placement, promotion, and supervision of the Afghans who worked for the agencies in question. As a result, at a time of rapid change and growing political discontent, the people who made up the most demanding sector of the Afghan population were divided on the bases of the foreign languages they used, the locales of their education and experience abroad, and their career avenues.[1]

Adding to the cleavages within the educated elite was the sociocultural distance between those who had been raised in the cities and their country cousins who had to compete with them. By the late 1960s students who had graduated from rural high schools were coming into Kabul in numbers that rivaled the production of Kabul's own secondary schools. The capital, with less than 5 percent of the total population, was beginning to be challenged by the rest of the country in the number of people who had access to higher education. The extreme concentration of cultural resources in Kabul clearly skewed opportunities for elite positions in favor of those who had been raised there. Rural newcomers were frustrated at every stage of their potential careers: university admission, competition for academic records, recruitment for government jobs and professional positions, career advancement. Ascribed identities—ethnic, religious, geographic, and linguistic—carried with them degrees of preference and discrimination. Some rural migrants benefited from elite networks based on membership in powerful tribal families, but prospects were limited for most of the rural people crowding into the cities.

Differences in degree of access to foreign-supported programs, ethnic group, and place of origin created a complex network of divisions among members of the expanding educated class. When these divisions were coupled with the overall shortage of opportunities for the newly educated as a whole, the danger of disaffection, scapegoating, and political rivalries among the educated became chronic. Accordingly, dissent became increasingly common, particularly within the rapidly growing student bodies of the secondary schools, teachers' academies, technical institutes, and the university.

The government had difficulty in finding means of channeling student energies away from political dissent. During both the constitutional period and Daoud's republican regime, the official policy toward student voluntary organizations was generally repressive. The political explosion that followed the street demonstrations over the naming of the cabinet in October 1965 continued to haunt the government. Given the limited means of venting their frustrations, students and unemployed graduates increasingly identified the royal family as the source of their troubles. In this situation it was easy for radical groups, both leftist and fundamentalist Muslim, to harness the discontent of the young for agitation against authority. On the campuses informal followings of Marxist spokesmen became increasingly fashionable (formal associations were illegal). Their ideological sophistication rarely seems to have gotten beyond sloganeering and posturing. Much of the left-wing agitation in the schools was directed at living conditions, quality of food, parietal controls—many of the features of school life criticized at one time or another by students everywhere. For the overwhelming majority of the young people involved, this was the first opportunity they had had to challenge any form of authority. To their surprise, agitation often brought concessions. Such successes and the experience gained in organizing campus demonstrations and strikes equipped leftist student leaders with skills they could later use to political effect. Tactically, they were ready to transform this experience from student agitation to political moves aimed at bringing down the government. Faced

57

with their own limited opportunities while the wealth of the favored grew more and more conspicuous, the radicals focused on government corruption and incompetence.

Discontent among the educated was also caused by conflicts between progressive and conservative views of education. The presence of female students in secondary and postsecondary schools presented special problems and pressures for the women, their families, and officials. The presence of women in public institutions brought opposition from religious leaders throughout the country and led to public demonstrations. These and other grievances on the part of the mullahs and other traditional leaders tended to polarize activist politics. The conservatives argued that rapid and massive doses of nontraditional education were leading to serious social dislocations and the démoralization of a large section of the country's youth. When their complaints were added to the conflicting demands of the Marxists, the liberal modernists who had designed the strategies for change found themselves on the defensive and unable to satisfy either side. The pace of change after 1960 had overwhelmed the plans and institutions established to develop the economy and the society. Ultimately events proved that clandestine organization and harassing techniques were the most devastating weapons available against an increasingly uncertain and confused government.

The Beginnings of Marxism

Marxism has prospered almost exclusively in the cities and among the young. In the circumstances confronting the newly and partially educated Afghans, their frustrations made them ripe for recruitment to a leftist cause. Nearly all Marxists were recruited on the campuses of the secondary schools and the teacher training academies. Older Marxists often retained their political connections even after they succeeded in getting government jobs. This process can be traced back only to the late 1940s. Before that, the number of students sophisticated enough to become politically active could be easily controlled by the government.

Students made their first demands for political and social change shortly after World War II. Their first organization, Youth for Reform, founded in 1948, helped to change the climate toward official acceptance of those who wished to reform the monarchy. The students of that time came almost exclusively from families of social and political prominence; accordingly, the government was sensitive to their demands. During the short period between 1949 and 1952, these elite students were given recognition by the government, even elected to the nominal national parliament. Many young reformers were extremely effective in articulating demands for a broadened government that would protect human rights and open the country to economic development. Many of their demands came to be recognized in government policy, but after Daoud came to power as prime minister in 1953, many students were treated as dangerous radicals and several served long prison terms. While most of these young idealists wanted socialist reforms that would redistribute wealth, almost none appear to have accepted a Marxist path for the future. This first generation of student reformers generally provided the foundation for the liberal changes that were attempted after 1963.

A few young idealists did later develop into Marxist ideologues. By far the most important was Nur Muhammad Taraki, a Pushtun of the Ghilzai tribe born south of Ghazni in 1917. The son of poor peasants, Taraki did not attend school beyond the elementary grades. Essentially self-educated, he eventually became a poet and a prolific writer whose fiction eventually was devoted to the cause of Marxist revolution.[2] Taraki appears to have first encountered Marxism while working as a clerk in Bombay in the 1930s. After his return home Taraki worked for government publication agencies throughout the 1940s. He was active in the student reform movement, although he was not one of its most outspoken leaders. In 1950 and 1951 he published a reform journal that was later suppressed. Yet he was assigned as press attaché to the Afghan embassy in Washington, D.C., in 1952. He resigned after a bizarre incident that is still disputed. After Prince Daoud became prime minister in 1953, Taraki called a press conference in a New York hotel and denounced the Afghan government as repressive and autocratic. The press reported his resignation and plan to seek asylum in Great Britain.[3] He embarked on an ocean liner the following day. Six weeks later Taraki emerged at the Afghan consultate in Quetta, Pakistan, to claim that he had been misquoted in the United States and that he was returning as a loyal Afghan to serve his government.[4]

Throughout his career as rebel and revolutionary Taraki displayed a tendency toward romantic egomania. His official biography reveals more about him than might have been intended. It reports that as soon as he returned from overseas, Taraki telephoned Prime Minister Daoud to say, "I am Nur Muhammad Taraki. I have just arrived. Shall I go home or to the prison?"[5] At the time he was not completely committed to revolution, but he insisted on making an impression. This determination to be noticed would surface in his sporting of a flamboyantly nonrevolutionary style of living after he gained political power.

Such controversy dogged Taraki over the next twenty-five years of his life. No longer employed by the Afghan government, he made his living by running a translation service that did business with the American embassy, USAID, and other foreign missions in Kabul. During the late 1950s he began to write radical fiction in which Afghan society was depicted as unjust and degraded. He became the center of a circle of radical writers and intellectuals but never was arrested or jailed, apparently much to his chagrin. Taraki's conversion to Marxism appears to have been gradual, but by the early 1960s he had begun to convert his younger followers to an ideological line that accepted the Soviet Union as the model for internal revolution and Soviet foreign policy as the blueprint that Afghanistan should follow. His Khalq followers claim that it was in Taraki's house in Kabul that the first meeting of the People's Democratic Party of Afghanistan (PDPA) was held in January 1965.

Two other Afghan Marxists were to prove crucial to the development of the revolution. Hafizullah Amin was born in the late 1920s of Ghilzai Pushtun parents near Paghman, in Kabul province. Also of peasant stock, Amin was born late enough to take advantage of the expansion of the secondary school system. A bright student, he was able to continue his education at Kabul University in the early 1950s, and in 1957 to win a scholarship for graduate study at Columbia University Teachers College in New York. He returned to Kabul with a master's degree and was assigned as principal to a boarding high school for rural Pushtun boys. He later was promoted to the principalship of Kabul's Teacher Training High School. His effectiveness as an administrator won him another scholarship to Columbia in 1963. To this point there is no indication that Amin was a committed Marxist. He was active in recruiting students on behalf of the Pushtunistan cause, championed by Prime Minister Daoud in the early 1960s.[6]

Amin's second residence in the United States came while significant political changes were being made at home. Suddenly open political activity became possible in Afghanistan. Amin became active in the Afghan student association in the United States. In 1963 he was elected president of the association, and he appears to have devoted most of his energies to running it, to the detriment of his doctoral studies at Columbia. Amin claimed to have been converted to Marxism at a student meeting in Wisconsin in the summer of 1963. Thereafter he devoted his efforts to radicalizing his fellow Afghan students. In 1965 he returned home after failing to get his degree and plunged into the Marxist politics of the PDPA.

Amin ran for a seat in the new parliament and was narrowly defeated. Taking a job in Kabul University's Institute of Education, he devoted his political energies to building the organization of the Marxist party. He proved to be a talented administrator and an effective recruiter. Accepting ideological guidance from Taraki, Amin became the organizing strongman of the Marxist group. Over the next few years he surrounded himself with young Pushtuns who had been radicalized by their school experiences and political ambitions. As a result, Amin developed a personal following within the organization and consequently considerable power. While he became a committed Marxist, his career demonstrated that his primary interest lay in developing personal political power. Ideology came second for him.

The major rival to Taraki and Amin within the PDPA was Babrak Karmal, a native of Kabul province and the son of an army general. Karmal received a modern education in Kabul and became caught up in the liberal student reform movement of the early 1950s. Jailed for several years by Daoud's first regime, Karmal emerged in the 1960s as the outspoken leader in the PDPA faction called Parcham ("Banner" in Persian). An eloquent orator, Karmal assumed the leadership of those radicals most closely identified with the Dari language and the emerging cosmopolitan life of Kabul. The Taraki/Amin wing of the party, which called itself Khalq ("Masses" in Persianized Arabic), was much more narrowly confined to Pushtun speakers. Karmal's ideological mentor was Mir Akbar Khyber, the Parcham theoretician who had been among the leaders of the reform movement of the late 1940s.

Despite some mild measures of repression, particularly through attempts to control the press, the constitutional government permitted opportunities for radical and other opposition groups to organize and gain support. While they were not permitted to organize legally, it was not difficult to build a political movement that could operate effectively on a semiclandestine basis.

The issues of unemployment, regulation of campus life, and royal corruption provided grist for the mill of Marxist recruitment. But as the PDPA grew, the gap between Khalq and Parcham widened, and by 1966 they were fierce competitors.

Beginning in 1966 Khalq published a newspaper, also called *Khalq*, which vilified the royal family and called for sweeping social changes, the expulsion of Western influences, and closer ties with the Soviet Union. Its demands were so strident that it was closed down by the government after five issues.[7] From that time on the Khalq faction became the more clandestine of the two. Parcham was more effective than Khalq in organizing support on the Kabul University campus, and it seems to have gotten more help from the Soviet Union to finance its operations. It is also possible that Parcham received encouragement and even some material support from Prince Daoud as he endured forced political retirement at his home in Kabul.

Parcham was by far the more active of the two organizations in the new parliament. Karmal and four of his Parcham colleagues had been elected in 1965 and used their offices to express constant criticism of the structure and the performance of the government. Their impact was multiplied by the lack of party organization and discipline within the parliament, which permitted their tightly organized cell often to dominate debate. Amin was elected to the parliament in the 1969 election and proved to be an effective spokesman for Khalq.

Parcham was also more fortunate with its publications. *Parcham* continued publication until 1969 and partly for that reason was accused by Khalq of being in complicity with the government. Differences in personalities, social origins, and tactics had widened the split between the two factions. The gulf widened further on July 17, 1973, with Parcham's success in carrying out the coup that brought it and Daoud to power.

The coup demonstrated that the Marxists had extended their operations from the campuses and streets of Kabul into the bases of the armed forces. The Parcham faction had been especially active in developing military contacts. As public discontent with the performance of the liberal government grew in the early 1970s, the Marxists were busy organizing cells in the officer corps and the civil bureaucracy. By the time Zahir Shah named Mussa Shafiq as prime minister, in December 1972, active conspiracies to overthrow the government were in progress. Some were concocted by non-Marxists interested either in reestablishing royal control or in bringing to power a more aggressive socialist leadership.

The Parcham conspirators fixed on Daoud as an ideal partner in their plans to seize control and develop a left-wing government. Daoud had always had close personal ties to the army. He had served as a lieutenant general before his elevation to the prime ministry. Though he had maintained close relations with the senior commanders throughout the period of his forced retirement, he appears to have had much less contact with the junior officers. They were now products of and influenced by the support and training they had received from the Soviets. Parcham's penetration and recruitment of strategically placed junior officers was to play a major part in the success of the coup. Coupled with Daoud's closeness to the senior officers, these military liaisons offered an excellent opportunity to ensure that the army would not oppose the removal of the king.

While Zahir Shah was in Italy for medical treatment, leaving Major General Abdul Wali, his son-in-law, to defend the government, the conspirators staged an almost bloodless coup. Key installations throughout Kabul were seized within a few hours; the only opposition came from police detachments that were not informed of the shift in authority. Official statements claimed that only eight persons died in the course of the transfer of power.

Daoud was named president of the republican government that was proclaimed the following day. He shared power with a revolutionary council whose membership was dominated by Parchamists, mostly young military officers. Khalq was virtually shut out of this republican government. Taraki and Amin accelerated Khalq's own attempts to penetrate the civil and military establishments in order to be in a position to seize power at some opportune moment.

The struggle between Daoud and Parcham for control over the republican regime has been described earlier. After Daoud had purged Parcham from the government, it found it prudent to return to an alliance, even if superficial, with Khalq. Jointly they planned a second coup, but it appears that each expected to seize power at the expense of the other. In the course of successfully executing the coup of April 27–28, 1978, Khalq in its turn shut out Parcham.

The history of the Marxist movement in Afghanistan before its seizure of power in 1978 is short and to a large extent obscure. Until 1973 Khalq and Parcham were splinter groups with limited and marginal support. The constitutional government under the king took the potential threat of the Marxists seriously enough to monitor their activities closely. Both factions were penetrated by government agents. The failure to crush the movement while it was weak was a reflection of the paralysis that afflicted the various cabinets in the last years of Zahir Shah's reign. It is likely that the government did not want to poison the political atmosphere by the arrest and suppression of active but apparently not very dangerous groups that were influential among students, many of whom had family ties with the political elite. Throughout this period Marxists gave the impression of dabbling in radical doctrine. It is certain that the Marxist movement's potential for mischief was underrated and the threat from Daoud misjudged. The general dissatisfaction with the slowness of the country's progress and the accumulating confusion over the goals and methods of bringing further improvements had largely immobilized the intellectual and political elite. In these circumstances the dedication of strategically placed Marxists to a program of subversion leading to a military seizure of power proved to be effective, not once but twice. Perhaps the most persuasive indicator of the political impotence of the active anti-Marxists was their acquiescence in these Marxist seizures of power. In the five years between Parcham's coup of 1973 and Khalq's coup of 1978 there was little or no evidence of a liberal or a democratic-socialist response to the threatened imposition of a totalitarian regime. If Afghan democracy was not quite stillborn, it died young and quietly.

4

The Khalq Regime,

April 27, 1978–December 27, 1979

Among violent seizures of power the Marxist coup must rank high in daring, execution, and luck. The complete and sudden success of the Khalq party after thirteen years of political irrelevance created a myth that obscured the political reality and made revolution difficult. Except for Khalq's experience at clandestine organization and intrigue, its leadership had virtually no qualifications for assuming control over a country. In its struggle to govern and to develop a coherent policy of revolutionary change, Khalq was further disadvantaged by its weak links with the Soviet Union, which had favored Parcham as the most likely instrument for revolution. The gulf between the Soviets and Khalq widened as the regime blundered into ever greater difficulties. As popular resistance against Khalq mounted, the Soviets concluded that the future of Afghan Marxism and their own influence were gravely threatened. The result was their invasion of December 27, 1979, and the execution of Hafizullah Amin, Khalq's surviving leader. Khalq rule therefore brought growing strife and incalculable damage to the Afghan social and political system.

This catastrophe was momentarily masked by the sudden success of the coup and the general acceptance of a radical but fresh leadership. While some religious leaders were quick to protest that a party officially committed to atheism had no place in the government of a Muslim nation, the bureaucrats, the educated elite, and even the commercial sectors of Kabul acquiesced in

Khalq's rule during the first few months. The early caution of the new regime contributed to its acceptance. In fact, the radical schemes to which Khalq was committed from the beginning could not be implemented for several months while it struggled for power with Parcham. With the expulsion of Karmal and other important Parcham leaders from the cabinet and their banishment abroad, Taraki and Amin were able to consolidate their power by late summer 1978. It was from that point that Khalq initiated the programs that were to produce an eruption of popular resentment. The honeymoon period following the coup was prolonged partly by the need to resolve the regime's own internal conflicts. Once that process was over, the effective leadership promised by the success of its coup proved to be an illusion.

The Coup of April 1978

Khalq succeeded in seizing power through tactics generally similar to those employed by the Parcham-Daoud coalition in 1973. A major difference in the circumstances was that the republican government was well aware of the danger and presumably had prepared itself accordingly. One result was that the struggle for power over thirty-six hours beginning on the morning of April 27 was immensely more costly and destructive than the earlier coup. The course of events was determined primarily by the advantages of initiative and surprise held by the conspirators and the confusion and almost incredible incompetence of the security forces that attempted to protect the regime. At several crucial points, lucky coincidence and timing played major roles.

In its official history of the coup Khalq claimed that responsibility for its planning was assigned to Hafizullah Amin as early as 1975.[1] At that time Parcham still had considerable influence in the republican government. Amin's task was to recruit air force and army officers who would mobilize units to seize centers of communication and control in order to paralyze the Daoud government. Its leaders could then be destroyed before the rest of the military and security establishment could move against the coup.

Amin's mission required the tedious and dangerous process of feeling out susceptible officers, persuading them to join the conspiracy, developing a specific plan of action, and perfecting its execution. All of these activities had to be carried out without discovery. In view of the number of individuals involved in frequent meetings, all of which had to be clandestine, over a period of more than two years, it is difficult to see how security agencies could have failed to be alerted. Circumstantial evidence points to the government's awareness of Khalq cells in the officer corps and of the plans for a political takeover. Its failure to take action is a mystery. Movement against the conspiracy was delayed too long. It is possible that government agents involved may have played double roles to be sure of being on the winning side.

The event that appears to have triggered Khalq's action was the assassination of Mir Akbar Khyber, a prominent leader of the Parcham faction, on April 17. His murderers have yet to be positively identified. Abdul Qadir Nuristani, Daoud's minister of the interior, had begun a policy of cracking down on left-wing radicals which could have led to the murder of Khyber. On the other hand, rumors persist that he was killed by his Khalq rivals.

Khyber's death set off a chain reaction that the Daoud government was unable to control. The two Marxist factions mounted demonstrations that spilled into the streets, mourning Khyber and defying the government. This was the first public demonstration against Daoud since his return to power. Some claims place the number of demonstrators at more than 10,000. Increasingly worried about the intensity of the protest, the government arrested the major Marxist leaders. Taraki was arrested at his home on the night of April 25–26 and was taken off to jail, apparently without a careful search of his papers. His wife was injured when she stepped between her husband and a bayonet-wielding policeman. Six others were arrested on April 26, including Amin, who was held under house arrest for several hours. According to accounts published by the Khalq government, during the time betweeen his arrest and his removal to prison the police suffered a lapse so remarkable as to invite speculation about collusion. While held in his home, Amin was permitted to write. He wrote instructions that told his confederates to begin the coup at eight the following morning. These instructions included a list of the names of some twenty young military officers involved in the plan for the takeover. They gave detailed directions on the armored and air force units that were to seize key government buildings and the Kabul airport and to block off units defending Daoud. The ultimate target was the presidential palace, defended by some 1,800 elite guards who could be expected to fight desperately and well. Under the noses of Amin's guards these instructions were taken from his house by his young sons and delivered to his fellow conspirators. Letting the children slip through their fingers, the Daoud officials lost their opportunity to nip the coup in the bud. Later that night Amin and other Marxist leaders were taken to jail. The fate of the coup was left to the young officers who had received Amin's messages.

In the face of the mounting street demonstrations, the army and government security forces had been placed on alert. But after the Marxist leaders were arrested, military units were ordered to celebrate the suppression of the leftists the following morning. This order greatly added to the confusion of the loyalist officers when they attempted to rally units in defense of the government.[2]

Shortly after eight on the morning of April 27, the rebel Fourth Armored Division began to move toward Kabul from its base at Puli Charkhi, south of the city. It met no resistance until after it arrived in the heart of the government district on its way to seize key buildings and to assault the palace. It was led by Colonel Muhammad Aslam Watanjar, who was to become one of the heroes of this revolution. After the armored division moved into the city, it helped Air Force Colonel Abdul Qadir to seize the airport. Qadir then flew a helicopter to Begram, forty miles north of Kabul, to take over the air force headquarters there. Assuming command, Qadir ordered the air strikes on the palace which were the turning point of the battle.

Meanwhile, joined by cooperating infantry units, Watanjar's Fourth Armored Division fanned out through the modern part of the city and gained control over key roads and intersections. It also seized the ministries of Communications, Foreign Affairs, and the Interior (the latter was the headquarters of the police and security forces). Throughout the day scattered battles occurred as rebel and loyal units confronted each other, often by accident and often without being certain whether they faced friend or foe. When the fighting started, General Ghulam Haider Rasuli, the army chief of staff, was at the palace. Trying to rally loyal units, he succeeded in breaking free from the palace, only to be painfully injured when his staff car ran a traffic light and smashed into a taxi.[3] He managed to get away but found it impossible to rally enough of his commanders. Many officers and their units wanted to wait out events before making a move to either side. Units of the Rishkhor Division did move into Kabul from the south and engaged in some fighting with the Fourth Armored.

In the early afternoon MIGs from Begram made their first passes at the palace. Until that time the presidential guards had held their own in hard fighting against the Fourth Armored Division. But under bomb and rocket strikes the defense of the palace broke down.

Earlier in the day Daoud ordered loyal units at Shindand Air Force Base, 500 miles to the west, to come to his defense. They arrived early in the afternoon, before the conspirators' attack from Begram. When they arrived, the Shindand planes had fuel for only ten minutes of flying time before they would have to return. During those crucial minutes they could not establish radio contact with the military command, and therefore could not identify the rebel units. They were forced to return home without dropping a bomb.[4]

This fiasco cost the Daoud forces their one real chance to turn the tide. In the late afternoon the tank forces broke into the palace courtyard and the surviving guards fled. Inside the palace, Daoud and some thirty members of his family congregated in a conference room. He appeared determined not to be taken alive. There are conflicting stories of how he met his death. One version claims that he fired on the troops that came to arrest him and died in a gun battle; in another version he shot himself after the troops had entered the room and then his brother, Muhammad Naim, started a gun battle in which many members of the royal family were killed.

By this time the rebels had seized the radio and television facilities, and from midafternoon they broadcast claims of victory. Loyal units continued to resist in and near Kabul until the next day, but lacking a leader and central coordination, most military units submitted to the victorious Marxists by the end of April 28. Khalq had been suddenly, violently, and spectacularly successful. Estimates of deaths from the fighting vary widely, from as few as 100 to 10,000; the most commonly accepted figure is around 2,000. The fighting around the palace had been fierce and a number of bloody encounters had taken place throughout the city. Among the casualties were many civilians who had unwittingly been trapped in the fighting. There were reports of large-scale executions of senior government officials and collateral members of the royal family in the days immediately following the coup, but later investigations suggest that such executions were limited to a few hundred. Kabul's second coup had been immensely more destructive than its first one, but the casualties were only a harbinger of the devastation that was to come.

On the afternoon of April 27, Taraki, Amin, Karmal, and other Marxist leaders were freed from prison. At the Ministry of Communications, Amin began to broadcast victory communiqués. Rivalries between these politicians were held in abeyance, but only temporarily. The exact roles of the two Marxist factions in the coup are still unclear. Later, after Khalq had purged the Parchamists, it was in a position to give the official account of what had happened. Not surprisingly, it accused Parcham of failing to cooperate and of counseling defeat, even of cooperating with the government. The Khalq government admits, however, that the two factions jointly took over the broadcasting facilities and that there was a degree of cooperation between them in the weeks immediately after they seized power.[5]

The Struggle for Power: May–July 1978

In the immediate aftermath of the coup, the Marxists organized a central revolutionary committee, which named Taraki president of the Democratic Republic of Afghanistan and prime minister of its cabinet. Amin and Karmal were appointed deputy prime ministers. The selection of the first cabinet suggests an attempt to achieve a delicate balance between the Parcham and Khalq factions: eleven ministers can be identified as members of Khalq and ten as Parchamists; the precise affiliation of the three military members is not certain, however, and several of the civilians appear not to have been fully committed to either group. The PDPA leadership formed an extraordinary in-group. Thirteen members of the cabinet had been founding members of the party. The positions given to Taraki indicate the dominance that Khalq had already established.[6]

The first weeks of the regime were deceptively quiet. In Taraki's first press conference, on May 7, he characterized the new regime as reformist, constructive, and tolerant of Islam. He pulled no punches about his hatred for Daoud and the former monarchy. He emphasized continuation of Afghanistan's nonalignment in international politics. But he insisted on calling himself the leader of a revolution, not a coup.[7] The conviction that the masses were behind them would lead Taraki and the clannish Marxist leadership to disaster.

Operating behind the public facade of the government was a thirty-five-member revolutionary council, whose membership has never been fully disclosed. A number of junior officers who played crucial roles in the coup served on the council, but it was dominated by Khalq stalwarts. From the beginning the Soviets were placed in an awkward position. They were linked far more strongly with the Parchamists than with the Khalq faction, both through government channels developed during the Daoud period and through support for agitation among students and intellectuals. At the center of this web of contacts was Babrak Karmal, whose eloquence in stating radical demands and vilifying the previous governments had won him a considerable personal following among Marxists. He was more visible than the older and less exciting Taraki, who had never been in parliament or in jail. Khalq entered its period of power with little popular backing. Its claim of 50,000 supporters at the time it seized power was a vast overstatement, probably by ten times the actual number. Its membership appears to have been limited to a network of students and recent graduates—often junior teachers in the government school system. Most were Pushtu speakers and therefore were identified with tribes and communities in eastern and southern Afghanistan. Khalq's Pushtun affiliations were further focused by the Ghilzai origin of most of its leaders. The Ghilzai tribe, the largest among the Pushtuns, had persistently opposed the royal government, which had been controlled by the Muhammadzai branch of the Durrani tribe. The Khalq leaders' animosity toward the previous government was partly founded on an ancient rivalry that was essentially tribal. Khalq was more clandestine and more tightly organized than Parcham, which had a more flamboyant leadership and a more open style of agitation. In the ensuing struggle for power, the cohesion and discipline of Khalq gave it crucial advantages. Neither side suffered from a lack of ruthlessness.

During its first three months the Marxist government committed few violent acts. It imprisoned or expelled surviving members of the royal family and their close retainers, it executed several Daoud cabinet members, and it removed a few senior bureaucrats and some eight hundred senior military officers. At this time the government contented itself with issuing broad and general directives on its foreign and domestic programs which stressed reform and continuity. Observers interpreted this mildness to mean that Khalq was in control of policy. Its later behavior would make a mockery of such interpretations.

Rumors of growing friction within the government preceded the dramatic announcement in late July that Karmal and five

Parcham associates serving in the cabinet had been assigned to ambassadorships. Karmal was sent to Prague. Since the assignment of cabinet members to the diplomatic service abroad had long been used in Afghanistan as a device to get rid of losers in a power struggle, this move indicated that Khalq was gaining exclusive control of the government. It was accompanied by the first of a series of purges of the middle and upper ranks of the armed forces and the civil bureaucracy. By November there had been three such waves of expulsions, and the remaining Parchamists were removed the following March. Many of these Marxists were imprisoned; the number executed is not known but is probably small. These developments left the Soviets in an uncomfortable relationship with the Marxist government they were committed to support. Khalq was establishing a reputation for being less revolutionary and more nationalistic than the more obviously Moscow-dependent Parcham.

Karmal and his senior colleagues did not enjoy their diplomatic sinecures for long. On October 1978 they were branded as traitors to the revolution and ordered to return home for trial. Prudently they remained abroad, where they were conveniently available to the Soviets when their patience with Amin ran out.

Khalq Policy and Performance

Popular acceptance of the Marxist regime lasted until the autumn of 1978. Many politically informed citizens interpreted the downfall of Parcham as the beginning of a nationalist and reformist era. Taraki and other government leaders were careful not to alienate Islamic sentiments. In the early weeks of the regime they attended Friday prayers in Kabul's mosques. Many of their proclamations were made in the name of Allah, and their announced reforms were accompanied by assurances that they would be consistent with Islamic law and teachings.

Taraki gained further popular acceptance by announcing a positive policy in regard to minorities in the first weeks of his regime. Virtually for the first time the official media used the Uzbek, Turkoman, and Baluch languages, and for the first time ever the government allowed publication of the works of the great Uzbek poets. Despite the strong Pushtun flavor of the new leadership, recognition of these minorities became official policy. The government intended to use cultural programs to win the allegiance of all minorities.

This period was marked also by declarations of intent to reform landholding, rural credit, marriage arrangements, and education. The policies that later emerged aroused explosive responses from the rural population, but the original declarations did not seem to be notably more drastic or threatening to the established rural order than had the rhetoric of Daoud's republic. Resentment awaited the actual materialization of these policies.

The last serious political obstacle to Khalq's control of the government was removed in late August, when Defense Minister Abdul Qadir, hero of the coups of 1973 and 1978, was suddenly arrested, ostensibly for attempting to bring Parcham back into power. With him were arrested Lieutenant General Shapur Ahmadzai, the army chief of staff, and the two remaining Parchamists in the cabinet, Lieutenant Colonel Muhammad Rafi and Sultan Ali Keshtmand, along with a number of minor figures in the government. After a period of imprisonment, they admitted the charges and were tried as traitors. Some observers believe that Qadir's crime was to object to growing Soviet control over the armed forces and Khalq's apparent willingness to lean on the Soviets for political support. Such complaints could have been justified by Amin's statement at the Third World Conference in Budapest that summer that Afghanistan considered its nonalignment to be consistent with membership in the Socialist camp, along with Vietnam, Ethiopia, Angola, and the Eastern European satellites.[8] Qadir's suspicions may also have been aroused by the decision to adopt the Soviet pattern of primary and secondary education and the introduction of Russian as a required foreign language for secondary students—in place of English. The latter move was a startling turnabout, for few of the Khalq leaders spoke Russian or had visited the Soviet Union before they came to power. Whatever the reasons for Qadir's removal, his elimination gave the Khalq leaders confidence that they could now enforce their policies for radical social changes.

Symbolic of the beginning of a new era was the declaration on October 19, 1978, that the national flag would be modeled after those of the Soviet republics. Most distinctive would be its color: solid red. The traditional Islamic green was nowhere to be seen. The government moved quickly to enforce the display of this symbol of revolutionary power everywhere in the country. Such an act was more than tactless; in one step it undid the months of pro-Islamic propaganda.

The unfurling of the red flag cannot be seen as an isolated case of misjudgment. Within a few weeks it was followed by declarations of sweeping reforms. The most important were (1) a policy of land reform designed to transfer 3 million acres of prime agricultural land from large holders to small holders and the landless; (2) the elimination of all usurious credit arrangements between moneylenders and the rural poor; (3) marriage regulations that reduced the customary bride price (which often reached as high as $1,000) to no more than 300 afghanis ($6), required the licensing of all marriages, and set the minimum age for marriage at 18 years; and (4) the introduction of mandatory education, based on a Marxist curriculum, for both sexes.

The announcement of these reforms did not raise an eyebrow. Afghans had heard similar rhetoric before. But suddenly people in small towns and the more accessible villages throughout the country found themselves confronted by a revolutionary officialdom, made up mostly of recent graduates from the high schools and the university, who impatiently insisted on immediate enforcement of the reforms. These young officials were backed by newly radicalized and well-paid police and ultimately by the armed forces, now controlled exclusively by a Marxist officer corps. For a people who had been able to ignore their government in most of their private activities in the past, it was a rude awakening. Any one of these programs, tactlessly introduced, would almost certainly have aroused a bitter reaction among most segments of the population. When they were introduced together as a package under the red banner of communism, the effect was catastrophic.

The attempt to implement the reforms led to an assault on traditional rural leaders. Khalq had already moved to kill off the most radical Muslim fundamentalists, the Ikwan-i-Musalamin, shortly after the coup. Now it began to arrest a growing number of secular and religious leaders throughout the country, and to execute them. In traditional Afghan political practice, arrests of local leaders were not necessarily considered to be cause for alarm. Previous governments had commonly taken leaders into custody as a way of exerting pressure to gain concessions. The Khalq regime, however, obviously had more drastic intentions. By the time the new reforms were introduced, in November 1978, a large number of local leaders had disappeared and many communities began to panic. Under such circumstances clashes between officials and ordinary citizens over any sensitive issue could easily bring about a sequence of obstruction, pressure, retaliation, wholesale arrests, assassinations, drastic repression, and popular revolt.

The government expected resistance but appears to have been trapped by its misreading of the nature of its own society. Before these radical changes were attempted, government spokesmen constantly repeated the theme that the new social and economic system would benefit the "98 percent" of the population that it claimed had no stake in the old order.[9] According to this logic, which Khalq apparently took literally, if the recalcitrant 2 percent could be brushed aside or destroyed, the majority would embrace government officials as deliverers from oppression. This insistence that its programs were designed to benefit virtually the entire population was to lend an air of fantasy to much of Khalq's propaganda. Its view of society forced the regime to interpret resistance as coming from a minuscule clique of religious and landed leaders, a few urban capitalists, and their misguided hangers-on. When it became obvious that 2 percent of the population could not account for the degree of resistance, the regime was forced by its own rhetoric to blame foreigners. First the Pakistanis and Iranians, then the Chinese and Americans were accused of stirring up internal strife.

This rhetoric involved more than propaganda. The claim of

77

foreign interference indicated a deep misconception of Afghan society. There is a particular irony here. Most of the Khalq leaders had rural backgrounds, yet they failed to recognize the inability of Marxist doctrine to explain the nature of their own society. To attempt to impose the concept of a hierarchy of social classes on a society as horizontally structured as Afghanistan's is the height of futility.[10] From their own personal experience Amin and Taraki and their fellow ideologues had to have been aware that it was often more important to know the family, clan, locality, language, tribe, sect, or ethnic community of a person they were dealing with than to know such class-related facts as the amount of land he owned or the trade in which he engaged.

The living standards of Afghans vary widely. The rich are extremely rich compared with the poorest farmers and nomads without land or animals. In some sectors of the country, notably in the fertile valleys, some families claim thousands of acres of private land. Comparatively great wealth also was amassed by the most successful of the banking and trading families. Individual members of the royal family also had extensive land and commercial holdings. A sizable number of the bureaucratic and commercial elite have amassed modest fortunes in real estate in and near Kabul. Yet the accumulated wealth of the tiny landed commercial elite has little bearing on the minimal subsistence conditions endured by many farmers and herders. Nor are differences in wealth heavily stressed in rural behavior and attitudinal patterns. Sensitivity to economic class differences is relatively recent. Before the twentieth century the struggle for survival and a measure of security was usually perceived in political terms. Groups fought for land and water. The economic results were usually seen in terms of ethnic competition. For example, the poverty of most Hazaras is partly the result of their failure to keep Pushtuns and Uzbeks from intruding into the central highlands for the summer grazing of their herds. A similar struggle went on between the Uzbeks and the original Tajik residents of the northeast. This struggle was aggravated by the arrival of government-supported Pushtun settlers early in this century. The Uzbeks gained control over the richest land in the lower levels of the Kunduz River basin, leaving the narrower upland valleys to the Tajiks, while the Pushtuns established low-elevation campgrounds and claimed rights in upland grazing lands, often in competition with the other two communities.[11]

Such intertwining of competing claims created the basic institutions of land control, agricultural operations, and herding throughout the country. There are many variations in the relative shares of power and benefits held by competing groups. The dominant realities behind social and economic relations are such political arrangements among groups. They determine the overall patterns of relative wealth and poverty within the population as a whole.

Within the communities themselves there are notable differences in wealth. Social values shared by nearly all Afghans strongly emphasize personal self-assertion. The demographic history of households is important for their economic status. The number of surviving children is crucial. The labor of able-bodied sons may permit a family to increase its landholdings or its herds. The bride price brought by a healthy daughter adds to her family's wealth. The failure to generate able-bodied children or a falling-out between father and sons or brothers could reduce a family's ability to keep its wealth. Rural politics is therefore closely identified with the struggle of household units to perpetuate themselves and remain unified.

This struggle is complicated by such external factors as vagaries in weather, epidemics of both animal and human diseases, and the displacements caused by migration and invasion. When such catastrophes occur, the weaker communities frequently find it necessary to retreat to inferior land, as in the case of the upland Tajiks. Population increase and the beginnings of commercialized agriculture have placed new pressures on the most fertile land in the lower valleys. Increasingly the weaker communities have been forced to accept dependent status as tenants, sharecroppers, or laborers of the groups that have gained control of a region. With the acceleration of competition among groups, patron-client relations across ethnic lines have become increasingly common. Even so, a large share of rural economic disparities is attributable to the relative abilities of households to compete within the same community.

Socioeconomic relationships in a segmented rural society tend to make local leadership extremely important. The families that cope best with their physical and social environments tend to become accepted as leaders by those less successful within the same community. While the mores of most groups stress equality and directness in relationships between peers, notable differences in economic and political status are recognized. An obligation that goes with wealth in the local context is the duty to lead and protect the less competent. There is a moral element in the titles given leaders. Indeed, ambition is intertwined with obligations to others in the code by which most traditional leaders live.

Exploitation has always existed in the socioeconomic system. Modern changes have provided new opportunities for the powerful and wealthy. Recent changes have been documented in the political-economic structure of nomadic groups undergoing transition to a partially settled life. Research north of the Hindu Kush discloses that the richer herding families have taken to buying expensive irrigated land. Meanwhile, as competition for grazing land becomes more fierce, the poorer nomadic families are losing their independence and becoming employees of the rich. In this sense, a spreading rural proletariat has begun to develop. In Marxist terms, the transition from feudal relationships attributed to tribal institutions is giving way to capitalist relationships between owners/employers and landless workers.[12]

As no complete survey of land use and ownership in the country has ever been undertaken, the published statistics on land tenure are sketchy, often contradictory, and generally unreliable. It is difficult to generalize about rural economic conditions beyond the impressionistic conclusions on land use offered above, but a majority of farmers and herders appear not to be hopelessly poor. In most communities small landholders who supplement their income with crops grown on land rented from others or with the products of self-replenishing herds are the most common. Their socioeconomic position is viable. Most people in most communities therefore accept the traditional order of things and give allegiance to a traditionally derived leadership, both secular and religious.

Despite these realities of rural life, the Khalq government was convinced that sweeping land reforms would win the support of the proletarian "98 percent." Its strategy was to eliminate the exploiting 2 percent by imprisonment, execution, or expulsion. A package of educational, social, land, and credit reforms would follow. Khalq's problem was that such a total program was certain to alienate nearly all elements of society, not just the alleged 2 percent. The government's impatience made the situation worse. It insisted that the whole program be put in force at once. Incredibly, there is no indication that pilot or model programs were attempted.

In November the government announced that some 3 million acres of land would be transferred to approximately 300,000 poor farming families. The following spring it claimed this task was completed. Although there is evidence that large amounts of land were taken from the largest holders, the confusion caused by the lack of preparation for such sweeping reforms is indicated by a one-third drop in the spring wheat harvest. Owners who feared expropriation had refused to plant their fields the previous fall. Many tenants were driven away so that owners could claim that members of their own families were cultivating the land. Islamic prohibitions against taking the property of others made many people reluctant to receive land. Credit dried up, since the landlords and large farmers who commonly supplied it feared to risk their money at a time of uncertainty. The government's assertion that the reforms were completed was an attempt to put a favorable light on the increasing difficulties of enforcement and the growing resistance of the peasants who were to receive land. [13] One is led to conclude that the immediate purpose of the reforms was to act as the cutting edge of a strategy to destroy the integrity of the social and economic relations that held rural communities together. By breaking relations between leaders and followers, the government expected to reduce resistance so that it could more easily remold society.

Mother and child, Bamiyan

While land reform was expected to turn the poor against the rich, traditional rural life was to be further shattered by enforcement of the new marriage regulations. The conventional arrangement called for payment of a bride price to the father of the bride. Customarily such a payment was considered to compensate the bride's parents for the services she would no longer render to them. In fact, the bride price is substantially reciprocated by household effects and clothing furnished by the bride's family. This system of exchange has frequently been used to cement political alliances or to end feuds. In such cases the bride may have little choice in the matter, but in the great majority of marriage arrangements the bride's feelings are taken into consideration when a husband is chosen for her. In introducing marriage regulations that reduced the bride price to a nominal fee and required a marriage license, the government was attacking the foundation of authority within the family and threatening the stability of relations between households. The reform can be interpreted as a noble effort to emancipate women, but the abruptness of its introduction reinforces the suspicion that its impact was intended to fracture the structure of the family and render the population more amenable to programs of social engineering.

Both the land reforms and the marriage regulations were violently resisted in the countryside. The confusion created by the land transfers created anxiety among farmers rich and poor, since it put so much arbitrary power in the hands of officials. Resistance to the marriage reforms was universal, since they affected all households, regardless of economic or political status. Hostility was also universal toward the changes in education. Shortly after Khalq came to power it announced revision of the national school system into a ten-year program modeled on the Soviet Union's. Russian was to replace English at the secondary school level. The furor over educational changes came before such innovations could be carried out, however. From the beginning Khalq indicated its determination to use the school system as the primary device for a fundamental and permanent Marxist reform of society. Its one area of strength in this regard was a group of radical young teachers who were available to indoctrinate their fellows in the revolutionary aims of the new curriculum. Non-Marxist teachers were soon persuaded of the wisdom of going along.

The government's intention to indoctrinate children with Marxist values could have been expected to lead to trouble. It was compounded by Khalq's insistence that all children now attend school. At the beginning of the regime, slightly more than half of the boys and barely one-tenth of the girls of elementary school age were enrolled in schools.[14] Marxist-influenced teachers, particularly young ones recently radicalized at the university or teachers' academies, now presented a threat to the authority structures and values of all Afghan communities with traditional lifestyles. The situation became explosive when local officials attempted to identify and enroll all children of school age. The willingness of most conventional rural families to allow their children to go to school had developed only since the late 1950s. The increase in the number of boys seeking enrollment led to a vast expansion of the national school system during the 1960s. Much of the criticism of the liberal constitutional governments of 1963–73 was directed at the inadequate staffing of local schools that had been built with labor and materials contributed by the communities. This enthusiasm for education (for boys) represented a revolutionary change in attitude. Education at the secondary level and beyond came to be perceived as a means by which a family could invest in its future prosperity. Since few career opportunities were envisioned for girls, the interest in providing them with anything but basic religious instruction was correspondingly less. Secular education for girls was embraced only by prosperous urban families and government officials. When Khalq forced the enrollment of girls in the schools, resistance could have been expected. Coupled with the prohibition of marriage before age eighteen, female Marxist education raised the specter of young women refusing to submit to family authority.

Taken together, these reforms virtually guaranteed opposition. Their enforcement by young, radical officials and teachers whose own outlook had been shaped by urban experiences and Marxist doctrines only added fuel to the fire. Beginning in the late fall of 1978, the impact of these reforms on the fabric of life was brought brutally home by government servants who saw no virtue in using tact or diplomacy. Incidents of protest quickly mushroomed into local armed revolts. Government officials became targets for assassination. The most self-defeating aspect of Khalq's program was its failure to give those elements of the population it championed anything they could recognize other than trouble. As a consequence, Khalq ignited one of the most truly popular revolts of the twentieth century.

In almost all cases resistance was a response by local communities to specific official acts. Yet isolated as the acts of resistance were, nearly all were directed at the atheism and Soviet domination of the government that was symbolized by its red flag.

Popular revulsion was unified in opposition to the treaty of friendship signed by the USSR and the Democratic Republic of Afghanistan on December 5, 1978. Modeled after Soviet treaties with Vietnam, Ethiopia, and Angola, this treaty linked the two patently unequal states in an intimate political, military, and economic alliance.[15] The change in the flag had demonstrated the regime's commitment to Marxism. The friendship treaty signified that the radical transformation of Afghanistan would be underwritten and guaranteed by Soviet power. By the end of 1978 the people had unmistakable evidence that their way of life could not survive unless they could manage to remove the Khalq regime. After that winter the virulence of the popular response overwhelmed Khalq's attempts at radical change. From then on the regime was forced to forget reform and concentrate on its own survival. During its last year in power the Khalq government became obsessed with its need to pacify the countryside. In this task it had increasingly to lean on its Soviet sponsors.

Khalq on the Defensive

By early 1979 the Khalq government faced a revolt that affected all but three or four of the twenty-eight provinces. The first indication that the opposition seriously threatened the regime came in Herat on March 22, after Pushtuns and Shias seized control of the city. Mobs hunted down all known Khalq officials and Soviet residents. Savage atrocities were committed. The insurgents maintained effective control over the city for three days before armored and air force units retook it in a bloody counterattack. There is some evidence that members of Afghan army units defected in the course of the fighting. Casualties from the fighting and the subsequent reprisals were extremely heavy. Some reports claimed at least 5,000 dead in a city with a population of some 85,000.[16]

The Herat uprising was the first urban challenge to the government. As almost all of Khalq's popular support was urban, control over the cities was essential to its survival. Soviet support and supply could ensure indefinite government control over the most vital and strategic roads, installations, and strongpoints only so long as the city populations remained supportive or passive. But Herat was not typical of Afghan cities: with a strong Shia minority, it was culturally oriented toward Iran, which by March 1979 had passed under the leadership of the Ayatollah Khomeini.

The Khalq government conveniently blamed Iran for the uprising. This charge was based on Iran's expulsion of many Afghans who had found work in the Iranian oil fields. Many of those workers were in the Herat area when the uprising began. The Khalq regime seized the opportunity to claim that the disturbance had been started by Iranian provocateurs. The factors operating in Herat may have been unique, but the episode demonstrated the urgency of maintaining control over the cities.

After Herat, opposition escalated in other regions. Attacks were reported on the major towns of Pul-i-Khumri, Mazar-i-Sharif, Kandahar, and Jalalabad. Jalalabad came under especially heavy pressure. In April Afghan soldiers mutinied when they were ordered to attack resistance groups near the city. They killed their Soviet advisers but were surrounded by loyal government units, reportedly reinforced by Soviet troops, and were defeated. In the confusion some of the mutinous soldiers defected to the resistance.

Government propaganda played down the incident as a barracks brawl. This event was followed in May 1979 by the first attempt at a large-scale attack when several thousand tribal troops attempted to capture Jalalabad. Inexperienced in large-scale combat tactics, they were routed by rapidly deployed armor and air assaults. Their failure provided the first demonstration of the limitations of large numbers of tribal warriors in an attack on a position defended by heavy air and ground firepower.[17] It is likely that some use was made of Soviet commando units at this time, just as it is possible that Russians may have aided in the defense of Herat. These episodes left the Khalq leadership badly shaken. A siege mentality developed.

The immediate aftermath of the Herat uprising was a sweeping reorganization of the Khalq government which brought

Amin close to effective control. Taraki remained as president of the republic and leader of the party, but Amin took over the prime ministership and began to assume control over the government agencies and departments.[18] Accompanying this shift was a final purge of the surviving Parcham elements in the cabinet, civil service, and the armed forces. Finding itself under an increasingly pressing siege, the Khalq leadership apparently decided that the remaining Parchamists could not be trusted, and many hundreds were jailed.

With the forming of a government of "national deliverance" on April 1, 1979, the Khalq leadership became even more dependent on the Soviets for military and economic support. By early summer at least 5,000 Russian advisers were in the country, about 1,500 of whom were military specialists assigned throughout the Afghan armed forces, down to companies of some 200 men. As the struggle became more desperate, Soviet units were attached to man MI-24 helicopter gunships and MIG-23s to increase the army's assault capacity. Despite these measures, the security of Kabul itself became progressively more questionable. The first visible demonstrations of opposition in the city came in late June and were easily suppressed. Then on August 4, an armored unit of the Afghan army stationed at Kabul's Bala Hissar fort mutinied and was crushed by massed planes and tanks. Throughout this period the heavily populated agricultural areas of the nearby Logar and Kohdaman valleys became the scenes of increasing resistance activity.

Foreign missions responded to these growing threats to the capital's security by evacuating most of their dependents. It was also reported that the immediate families of Taraki and Amin were temporarily evacuated to the Soviet Union, and that the government ministries of greatest security sensitivity were being evacuated to military compounds in or near Kabul.[19] These developments served as indicators of waning confidence in the ability of the Khalq government to survive.

Diplomatic observers in Kabul repeatedly suggested that the Soviets were becoming increasingly disillusioned with the policies and performance of the Khalq regime. The Soviets had counseled caution in the implementation of the reform programs launched the previous fall, and when popular hostility became unmistakable, their doubts about the viability of the government grew. Some consideration was apparently given to the appointment of non-Marxists to the cabinet as a political device to win over the secular resistance groups. While the hardline religious insurgents could not be expected to be mollified by any government gestures, the Soviets hoped that some of the tribal and minority ethnic groups might accept a broadened government. Nothing was to come of this idea, probably because of the opposition of Prime Minister Amin, whose control over the inner workings of the government was becoming total. This situation produced friction between him and President Taraki, who was willing to accept a softer line. The Soviets appear to have seen an opportunity to eliminate Amin by supporting the Taraki faction.

Taraki made his move on the weekend of September 14–16, 1979, immediately after his return from the Conference of Nonaligned Nations in Cuba. On his way home from Havana, Taraki had spent at least two days in Moscow, where he was enthusiastically received by Brezhnev. There are reports that Karmal and perhaps other Parchamists were present at their talks. By this time Taraki must have been disturbed by Amin's relentless drive to take total power. The Soviets and the Parchamists in exile could have offered him an opportunity to outmaneuver Amin and to reorganize the government along softer lines.

Probably armed with assurances from the Soviets that they would move quickly to reinforce an attempt to remove Amin, Taraki returned to Kabul and attempted a coup of his own. The key to its success was to be the assassination of Amin as he entered the presidential palace for a cabinet meeting summoned by Taraki. But Amin's bodyguard, who may have been informed of the plot, took the shots intended for his boss. Amin escaped and rallied the guard unit in the palace to his defense. In the ensuing shootout an unknown number of cabinet officials and senior party members were killed or wounded. Amin emerged in control.[20] Several days later the government announced that Taraki had died of an undisclosed illness.[21] Amin had satisfied his ambition of gaining total control of the Marxist movement in Afghanistan. His success came at the cost of a rift with the Soviets which ultimately could not be healed. Their penetration of the army and air force through their network of advisers seriously limited Amin's freedom of action. As long as they concentrated on suppression of the resistance, however, the rivalry did not break into the open.

There was growing evidence that the Afghan army was disintegrating. It had been severely affected by the purging of large numbers of officers who were apolitical or suspected of Parchamist connections. Soviet military advisers were assigned to fill the gaps. As army personnel became demoralized and the command structure politicized, guerrilla forces increasingly gained the initiative and attracted defections.

The government tried to offset these losses by recruiting recently educated youths who presumably supported the regime. Many students and recent graduates living in Kabul may indeed have backed Amin, but their ability to fight in rural areas was questionable. Attempts were made to overcome this problem with communist indoctrination and the protection of armored and aerial equipment presumed to be capable of decimating the opposition in the open countryside.

An ambitious campaign was launched in late October against Pushtun tribal insurgents near the Pakistan border. Although the resistance fighters were scattered and suffered heavy casualties, it was clear within a few weeks that such lightning blitzes with air and armor had not substantially changed the situation. The road system was coming increasingly under the control of the insurgents and their power was growing in the immediate vicinity of Kabul itself. These pressures were accompanied by a final breakdown in Amin's relations with the Soviets. In early October his foreign minister complained bitterly to an assembled group of Eastern European diplomats of Soviet "unreliability and treachery."[22] There were clear signs that the Afghan military was once again choosing sides on the question of who should control the government.

In December the final impasse was reached between Amin and his Soviet allies. Surrounded by enemies, even among his Marxist colleagues, Amin had turned to his close relatives to fill the most vital jobs in his beleaguered government. In a curious throwback to the traditional system of Afghan statecraft, this avowed Marxist had appointed his nephew, Asadullah Amin, as chief of the secret police. Asadullah was fatally shot in mid-December; his assailant has not been disclosed. Unnerved, Hafizullah Amin moved his headquarters to the Darulaman Palace, on the outskirts of Kabul, reportedly on the advice of General Viktor S. Paputin, a senior KGB officer sent by the Kremlin as an envoy in early December. The move initiated the last phase of Amin's downfall. He died in the palace under disputed circumstances. There are reports he was poisoned by cooks furnished by the Russians. He may have died before a Soviet parachute unit attacked the palace and forced Amin's guards to surrender. All sources agree he was dead after the assault was over. Paputin also died mysteriously, either in the assault on the palace or, it is rumored, by his own hand. In any event, the Soviets had now positioned themselves to arrange for a transfer of power.[23] The Khalq experiment had been a disastrous failure, with consequences that not only were devastating for the country, but would swiftly bring about a global crisis.

5

The Resistance

Violent resistance to the Khalq government was general in its extent but local in its origin. By early 1979 virtually no part of the country was secure except for the major cities. Yet the revolt was fragmented. It was conducted by local groups that rose in defiance of provincial officialdom. In order to survive, the insurgents had to mobilize for indefinite armed conflict. They had no unified leadership. The scattered and isolated character of the revolt is the most fundamental fact about it. Its common denominator is hatred of official policy and behavior. What the insurgents share is a revulsion against symbols of an atheistic and Soviet-dominated regime.

Attempts to unify or coordinate the resistance have faced great obstacles. Its social basis is the primordial group—the household, the extended kin group, the clan, the subtribe or tribe, often the hamlet or valley neighborhood or sectarian community. When operating as guerrilla units, such groups have been able to rely on their established internal structure of authority and discipline. Thus the resistance has frequently been organized and led by the traditionally respected and powerful members of the group. Yet it has also been common for lesser members to come forward to lead revolts.

Inevitably, the fragmented resistance movement has been divided along regional, ethnic, and sectarian lines. Local groups have coordinated their activities only within the limits of distinct regional or linguistic communities. Most prominent in this respect have been the Nuristanis, Badakhshanis, Hazaras, and the numerous Pushtun tribes.

91

In the course of Afghan history, especially in the twentieth century, these major groups have rarely been on friendly terms. In the competition for favorable relations with the government, the leader of the regional groups have almost always seen each other as rivals. Their rivalry has been compounded by the dominance generally achieved by the Pushtun communities.

The struggle against the Kabul government has been carried out largely by country people, little touched by modern experience or education. Educated urbanites have been slower to join the resistance. Until the spring of 1980, opposition in the cities had predominantly involved traditional minority communities, such as the Shias of Herat and Kabul.

The educated class occupies a particularly vulnerable position in this struggle between the center and the countryside. It is hard for an educated city man to participate in an essentially rural war. While individuals and families with advanced education may have strong personal roots in the villages, many such roots have been cut in the last generation. Few of this class are in a position to commit themselves openly to the cause of their rural cousins because their activities are under constant surveillance. In effect the nature of the civil war has politically emasculated most of the educated middle class.

Since 1978 at least ten resistance organizations have established headquarters in Pakistan. Their leadership and ideological programs represent a wide spectrum of Afghan society and political ideology. From the beginning they have found it difficult to cooperate with each other or to give effective support to the groups fighting inside the country. These resistance organizations have competed for international support in order to acquire the military supplies necessary to carry on the war. Success in gaining such support requires effective publicity. Their rivalry in gaining the attention of Muslim and Third World nations has been especially sharp. At the beginning their disunity limited their effectiveness. Later, after the Soviet invasion, the émigrés started to pull together.

The organization that made the first effort to bring all resistance activities together was the Afghan National Liberation

Front, under the leadership of Sibghatullah Mujadidi. The Front was founded in the spring of 1978, just after the coup, with the support of Muslim intellectuals from Saudi Arabia and other Persian Gulf states.[1] A long-time opponent of Daoud, who jailed him in the 1950s, Mujadidi remained abroad during Daoud's republic as director of an Islamic studies center in Denmark. This position and his reputation as a modernist Islamic scholar gave him opportunities to pull together international support for a unified resistance movement. In the fall of 1978 Mujadidi's National Liberation Front established headquarters in Peshawar, Pakistan, and since then he has attempted to bring together the frequently squabbling leaders and organizations that claim to speak for the Afghan resistance.

As a resistance leader Mujadidi has impressive credentials. He is a member of the family of the Hazrat Sahib of the Shor Bazaar in Kabul, which developed a network of Islamic devotional centers in the major cities. The Mujadidi family has long been associated with the Nakshbandi order of Islamic devotionalism, in the Sufi tradition. During the nineteenth century one line of the family rose to prominence among scholars in north India. It became established in Afghanistan after World War I, when the Hazrat Sahib founded a center at Kabul. After opposing Amanullah's reforms, the Mujadidi family became prominently involved in the royal (Musahiban) government. It also became increasingly identified with modernist reforms. In the 1950s the family ran afoul of Daoud, who disliked any form of political independence that might threaten his power.

Sibghatullah Mujadidi inherited a family legacy that could provide him a base for a broad national following. He can be identified with a cross section of the movements and ideas, reformist and nationalist, which are capable of rallying modern Afghans against Marxism. These modernist credentials, coupled with his religious stature, ensure him a receptive audience among the conservatives. Mujadidi's National Liberation Front occupies a moderate place within the ideological range of resistance groups headquartered in Pakistan.

The organization that originally had the largest number of

93

mujahidin (Muslim holy warriors) under its leadership was the Islamic Revolutionary Front of Sayyid Ahmed Effendi Gailani. Gailani is also an Islamic moderate with a distinguished family background of religious scholarship. His family, which originated in Baghdad, established the position of *pir*, or spiritual teacher, among several Pushtun tribes in the Paktia region, immediately adjacent to the Pakistan border. Receptive to modern reforms, Gailani attempted to cooperate with the Khalq government in its early weeks. He fled Kabul when he realized how crude and doctrinaire its Marxist program was.[2] Having established a resistance headquarters in the loosely administered tribal zone of Pakistan adjoining Paktia, Gailani was strategically placed to inspire and guide his tribal followers. He has political influence over a sector of the population of great potential military importance, in contrast with Mujadidi's limited personal contact with groups engaged in the fighting. While their ideological positions are similar, the differences in their personal situations and sources of support have made it difficult for them to unite their movements.

The émigré group most resistant to unification or joint policies has been the Hizb-i-Islami, or Islamic Party, of Gulbuddin Hekmatyar. A former engineering student who completed two years at Kabul University, Hekmatyar gave up his studies to join the Ikwan-i-Musalamin's resistance against Daoud's government. He participated in an abortive attempt to start a rebellion in the Panjshir Valley and afterward fled to Pakistan, where he founded the Hizb-i-Islami. Born in rural Wardak province, Hekmatyar is one of the youthful leaders who are determined that the changes that accompany modernization must conform with the tenets of Islam. Despite his comparative youth (he is in his early thirties), Hekmatyar's eloquence and organizational ability have attracted a wide following among both the rural Pushtun population and educated city dwellers, many of whom have escaped to join his movement.

This group has developed from a cadre of religious conservatives who fled Daoud's regime after 1973 and organized themselves into an armed strike force with the aim of seizing power and creating a fundamentalist political system that would tolerate no political rivals. Hekmatyar's group is an offshoot of the Afghan branch of the Muslim Brotherhood, led by Muhammad Niazi, which attempted to attack the Daoud republic from within and was repressed. The Hizb-i-Islami consistently holds itself aloof from the other émigré organizations. Hekmatyar has attempted to cultivate political support among conservative Muslim groups in revolutionary Iran. He has claimed that his rivals are too close to either the royal family or the Western bloc. Despite his organization's total opposition to Marxism, Hekmatyar has attempted to carve out an independent position so as to be potentially acceptable to all parties, including the Soviets, should a political compromise leading to a neutralized Afghanistan become feasible. The Hizb-i-Islami has developed the most effective of the émigré press campaigns in its efforts to proclaim the feats of its mujahidin in the war.

Also conservative but more accommodating toward its rivals is the Jamiyat-i-Islami, led by Burhanuddin Rabani. This group also aims to establish a government based on a literal reading of Islamic law, but it would permit an openly competitive political system in which modernists could participate. Rabani is a fundamentalist theologian, formerly a professor in the faculty of Islamic law at Kabul University. His personality and ability to get along with competing politicians has made him one of the most effective of the resistance leaders operating in Pakistan. His organization has benefited from the support of the Pakistani Jamiyat-i-Islami, which achieved great influence under the leadership of the late Maulana Maudidi. Unlike Hekmatyar, Rabani has been willing to cooperate with Mujadidi's National Liberation Front.

Other émigré organizations include the Islamic Revolutionary Movement, under the leadership of Malawi Muhammad Nabi, and the Shola Jowid, a Maoist splinter group that escaped after the April 1978 coup. A number of spokesmen for regional groups carrying on active resistance inside Afghanistan also have their headquarters in Pakistan, where they attempt to muster aid in redressing their particular minority grievances. Representives of the Hazaras, Badakhshanis, Uzbeks, Nuristanis, and Baluch have agreed to associate with Mujadidi's National Liberation Front.

Until they mastered the vital problems of supplying and coordinating the fighting inside Afghanistan, the émigré organizations could not expect to exert significant political influence on the guerrillas. Their influence depended on their effectiveness in funneling foreign aid to the mujahidin. A crucial question was whether, in the event that supplies should become abundant, the émigré organizations would be able to apportion them evenhandedly among the fighting groups. If they could, a united expatriate leadership could obtain growing control over the whole resistance movement. Supply and coordination could then eventually provide a foundation for a credible government of national liberation. The role of the émigré leadership, therefore, could significantly expand.

The Emergence of Resistance

Resistance to the Khalq regime did not develop until it became clear that the government was taking its revolutionary rhetoric seriously. In the first few months Taraki's insistence that the Khalq party did not intend to pursue drastic measures and his refusal to permit his regime to be identified as communist had a calming effect on most sectors of the population. His release of political prisoners held by Daoud was a popular move. A number of moderate politicians, particularly those who had supported former prime minister Muhammad Hashim Maiwandwal (1965–67) and who had suffered under Daoud, were willing to work for the new regime. During the first few weeks of government reorganization, while Khalq and Parcham were maneuvering for control, relatively little criticism was heard.

Vocal attacks on the government as atheistic and anti-Islamic did come from the Ikwan-i-Musalamin (Islamic Brotherhood). It is likely that at that time the Brotherhood's leader, Muhammad Niazi, who had been jailed by Daoud, was executed by the Marxist government. This partly clandestine organization then

Nuristani man, Faizabad

went more deeply underground. Its survivors claim that they organized a "rescue front" that launched sporadic attacks on government officials, military installations, and stray Russians. It was later to take credit for uprisings in several provinces.[3] The Brotherhood's activities were suppressed, however, and its adherents were either killed or driven from the country. Its role in later resistance activities, which were carried out almost entirely by local and regional groups, remains unclear.

The first of the regional groups to make their opposition known were the Nuristanis, in the mountainous country north of the Khyber Pass. The Nuristanis have never fitted comfortably within the modern Afghan political system. Divided into five major tribes, they occupy the upper reaches of the Kunar River basin, whose ridges and peaks frequently reach more than 17,000 feet. In this rugged territory the Nuristanis have developed an independent culture whose origin is disputed. Their usually light hair and blue or gray eyes have prompted suggestions that they are descended from the soldiers of Alexander the Great. Whatever their beginnings, for centuries the Nuristanis maintained a lifestyle that distinguished them from all other peoples in the country, especially with regard to religion. They were forcibly converted from polytheism to Islam just before the turn of the twentieth century. Despite their conversion, the Nuristanis have remained a people apart.

They long had grievances against the central government, whose local and provincial officials were almost invariably Pushtuns. For several generations since their conversion and absorption into the national political system, they have felt at a serious disadvantage in matters of justice, taxation, and economic competition.

In order to cope with these pressures, the Nuristani khans found it necessary to provide two types of service for their people: internal and external. They attempted to maintain internal autonomy by regulating and mediating affairs within the community. The mark of success in this respect was the successful maintenance of harmony and consensus within and among villages. But this task became increasingly complicated by the need

The Kunar Valley

to cope with the intrusions of external authority, personified by
the provincial governor and his staff, particularly the police.
Since Nuristanis were virtually excluded from such offices, the
khans' responsibility was to maintain as effective a shield of isolation as possible against tax collectors and other vexations. The
most critical areas of outside interference involved law, public
education (not carried out in their language), and development
projects that threatened their control over the land and forests.[4]

Such interference gave them ample reason to remain isolated.
Yet a degree of protection had been developed at the highest
level by relations of direct patronage between the khans and the
royal court. Since Nuristan occupied a strategic position on the
border with British India (later Pakistan), the monarchy had
reason to be sensitive to its political situation. Nuristanis were

therefore recruited into the central military forces. Under Daoud's republic several Nuristanis held senior ranks in the armed forces and the police. Daoud counted on them as an inner circle of defense against threats to his regime.

The Nuristanis' history of friction with neighboring Pushtun tribes and their visible role in the republican government made them targets for persecution as Khalq sought to win popularity with their neighboring rivals. After the coup, several leading Nuristani military officers were executed by the new regime and Nuristani leaders who had mediated between the community and the government were arrested. In retaliation, Nuristanis attacked police and minor government outposts in the Kunar Valley in the summer of 1978. During this early period of Khalq rule the regime attempted to enlist traditional hostility against the Nuristanis by arming their Gujar neighbors, and even tried to invoke a jihad (holy war) against them as infidels, despite their devotion to Islam. An assortment of Gujar and Pushtun tribal auxiliaries and police units were sent against them, with little success. The government bombed some of their wooden villages, which are often exposed along the ridge lines. These tactics forced abandonment of some villages as the communities scrambled to higher ground during the warm weather. The casualties caused by the bombing did not weaken their ability to resist.

Their location adjacent to the border simplified the process of buying arms in Pakistan, but shortage of supply largely restricted their purchases to outmoded hand weapons. Even so, by early fall they had consolidated their positions throughout the upper valleys of the Kunar basin. They had driven off the government auxiliaries and fought army units to a stalemate at the key valley town of Chigha Sarai. In effect, they had fought their way to political autonomy within their own mountains and valleys, and so long as the border of Pakistan provided a means of supply and escape, their tactical advantage was beyond the army's ability to overcome.

Limited as it was, the struggle for Nuristan became the prototype for regional uprisings and Marxist responses elsewhere.

The two most active of the other regional groups have been the mountain Tajiks and the Hazaras. These Tajiks, whose home is in the most remote valleys and mountains of Takhar and Badakhshan provinces, in the extreme northeast, live in an environment similar to that of the Nuristanis. They also have experienced a recent history of interference and oppression at the hands of their ethnic neighbors. They lost many people to the conquests and resettlement policies of the Uzbek chiefs in the nineteenth century. Many of them were forced into the highest inhabitable valleys of the region, while Uzbeks and later Pushtuns took over the more productive and comfortable lowlands. Oppressed and despised by their neighbors, they now rose against a Marxist revolutionary government that promised reforms to benefit the poorest and weakest elements of the population. As the Tajiks have been in constant contact with their cousins across the border in Soviet Central Asia, they have firsthand knowledge of Marxist rhetoric and Soviet deeds.

The Tajiks were already sensitive to Pushtun domination. Faizabad, the capital of Badakhshan province, had become largely a Pushtun settlement in the twentieth century, surrounded by valleys tilled by Uzbeks and Tajiks. When the officials of the Khalq government brought the gospel of radical reform, their activities were seen as a new wave of Pushtun interference rather than as an effort to bring deliverance to the toiling masses. Late in the summer of 1978 Tajik-dominated resistance groups denied large sections of the region to government troops and besieged Faizabad.

A similar set of circumstances brought similar results to a large part of the Hazarajat, the central highland region. The Hazaras are the largest group that has been consistently oppressed by the Pushtuns. Like the Nuristanis, the bulk of the Hazara population was not brought under effective central control until the 1890s. Since that time their ability to subsist in their arid mountains has become progressively more difficult. Nomadic groups—Pushtun, Uzbek, Turkoman—have taken over highland pasturage and used the profits from the merging networks of modern trade to buy up some of the best irrigated land.

Faizabad, from across the Kokcha River

These developments have forced a growing proportion of the Hazara labor force to emigrate seasonally to the cities, particularly to Kabul, to look for unskilled work. Their distinctive Mongol appearance and their association with the Shia branch of Islam have caused them to be treated as inferior. Popular folklore has them descended from the despised conquering hordes of Genghis Khan. When local Khalq officials, mostly Pushtun, abruptly introduced reforms, there was yet another minority reaction. By the autumn of 1978, Hazara groups and government forces were fighting at the beautiful and historic town of Bamiyan, the northeastern gateway to the Hazarajat. The Hazaras followed the familiar pattern of sealing off remote areas from government penetration, leaving them vulnerable only to bombing attacks.

As a result of the resistance by the Nuristanis, Tajiks, and Hazaras, a large part of Afghanistan came under the control of minorities. These uprisings generally took the form of guerrilla attacks against officials and police detachments in the smaller towns and disruption of traffic on difficult country roads. Such operations weakened government control and rekindled traditional impulses to plunder. While the amount of territory they controlled was impressive, the defiance of these minority peoples presented little threat to the Khalq government in Kabul. The hostilities involved a small proportion of the population and did not affect the prosperous sectors of the country. But they set a pattern of resistance that would later spread.

Resistance greatly accelerated in the fall and winter of 1978–79, when the Khalq government attempted to carry out its agrarian, social, and educational reforms. As we have seen, these policies aroused anger and fear in all quarters. The new flag and the friendship treaty with the Soviets, which effectively put the fate of the government in Soviet hands and the country within the Soviet bloc, galvanized opposition among all rural groups, even the Pushtuns. No previous government had survived without strong Pushtun support. From late 1978 the isolated campaigns spread until they involved all sections of the population, including many in the cities.

Several major Pushtun tribes—the Waziris, Mohmands, Afridis, and Yusufzais—recognized danger to themselves in the Soviet treaty and, under the leadership of Sayyid Ahmed Gailani, joined in a jihad against the Khalq government. They were aided by their proximity to the Pakistan border, which is virtually unsealable and provided both refuge and supplies, as the Nuristanis had already demonstrated.

In December, Mujadidi's National Liberation Front announced the creation of a coalition of émigré groups headquartered in Pakistan. The Hizb-i-Islami was the most prominent exception. The coalition was to be based on a moderate consensus on the goals of national liberation. Its manifesto promised material and social progress consistent with Islamic socialism and a prominent role for religious leaders.

> The Afghan National Liberation Front strongly believes that the sincere and true application of Islamic principles is the only way to ensure the survival and well-being of our nation. Therefore, we shall struggle for the establishment of a government founded on Islamic teachings and our own traditions of democracy.
>
> . . . The ANLF . . . opposes emphatically the re-establishment of one man or one party dictatorship depriving our people of their right to self-determination.
>
> ANLF will fight against ethnic discrimination, class distinction, economic exploitation in Afghanistan, and will strive for establishment of an economic and social order consistent with the Islamic concept of social justice.
>
> ANLF will fight for the protection of individual rights, the right to live, the right to be free, the right to equality before justice, the right to equal opportunity and the right to personal property.
>
> ANLF will fight all elements of imperialism and feudalism which hinder the establishment of a politically independent, economically prosperous, and socially progressive Afghanistan.
>
> ANLF . . . will re-establish, according to Afghanistan's traditional policy, a true and constructive neutrality.
>
> . . . May God lead us into victory over atheism, treason and national slavery in our land. May He help us to establish a true Islamic society founded on freedom, justice, equality and the brotherhood of man in our own interest and the interest of the international community.[5]

This announcement paralleled a wave of resistance against the government which spread across the whole country. From this point on, the government was challenged in all regions by guerrilla resistance. But the resistance groups lacked the political and tactical capability of waging large-scale warfare.

The government retaliated with alternate concessions and reprisals that had little effect on the resistance. In January 1979 the government launched a concerted crackdown on religious leaders, including an assault on the offices of the Hazrat Sahib of the Shor Bazaar in the old city of Kabul, the Mujadidi family's religious headquarters. Reportedly more than 120 people were arrested and many executed in these assaults.[6] They marked the beginning of a general war on all important religious leaders throughout the country. Survivors joined the resistance or fled the country. Those who fled were often accompanied by followers. The repression of religious institutions added greatly to the fervor of the resistance.

In early February came the tragic and still unsatisfactorily explained kidnapping and killing of the American ambassador, Adolph Dubs. An armed gang stopped his car on the way to the U.S. embassy, captured him, and took him to the Kabul Hotel. There Dubs and his captors were all killed in a "rescue mission" carried out by the Afghan police under the direct supervision of a senior Soviet security adviser. American attempts to dissuade the Afghan authorities from attacking the kidnappers were disregarded. The official explanation given was that the kidnappers were members of an ultrafundamentalist Shia group. The gang allegedly demanded the release of a large number of prisoners who belonged to a Tajik religious minority. Dubs's death, like the deaths of Habibullah, Daoud, Amin, and Taraki, will probably never be adequately explained.

This incident had an indirect impact on the political situation inside the country. Until this time, American policy had been to ignore the Khalq government's alliance with the USSR. The United States had faced a dilemma. The USAID program in Afghanistan was one of its largest. Major projects continued in agriculture, education, public administration, population policy, and industrial development. By law, American aid could not legally be given to countries classified as communist. The State Department had simply ignored the actual situation, continued to fund existing programs, and provided no encouragement to the resistance against the Marxist government. With Dubs's murder, American assistance was brought to an abrupt end. The staff of the American embassy was sharply reduced and Ambassador Dubs was not replaced. Relations between the United States and Afghanistan were reduced to the minimum formal correctness. Soviet and official Afghan recognition of this change was marked shortly thereafter by accusations that the resistance was being inspired, supplied, and even conducted by Americans (presumably in concert with the Pakistanis, Iranians, and Chinese who had already been publicly blamed).

With the end of winter, resistance activity flared into unprecedented intensity. Fighting spread to nearly all provinces and was highlighted in late March by the uprising in Herat.

During its last six months the Khalq government suffered increasingly from military mutinies and piecemeal defections by individual soldiers, officers, and small units. The most dramatic episode occurred on August 6, when a tank unit stationed in Kabul mutinied and temporarily got control over a part of the Bala Hissar Fort, which served as a camp and ammunition depot. Its suppression took several hours of armored and aerial bombardment. Similar but less well-documented breakdowns in discipline and outright resistance to the regime occurred among army units elsewhere. In the confusion it became clear to Amin that his Soviet military advisers were conspiring against him. He became increasingly isolated from and fearful of the military forces protecting his regime.

The last major campaign conducted under Amin's leadership was directed at a large concentration of Pushtun tribal contingents in Paktia province. Two insurgent headquarters were seized in a combined air and ground assault in late October. The campaign appeared to be an immediate success, since it scattered the resistance forces and sent a new wave of refugees fleeing to Pakistan. But the armored forces and infantry could not be supported effectively so far from the main roads, and as they were pulled back, the Pushtun groups were able to reclaim their positions. After this substantially abortive effort, the military posture of the government became essentially defensive. As winter closed down much of the fighting, the prospects for the regime appeared bleak at best. During the last half of 1979 the resistance had grown and become better organized. Larger concentrations of better-equipped insurgents could be expected to wage increasingly more aggressive battles against the government in 1980. Under these circumstances, Amin prepared himself for a final siege. The Soviets were forced to decide how much they wished to pay in military costs, manpower, and world opinion to dominate Afghanistan.

6

The Soviet Invasion
of December 1979

Finding that milder means had not allowed it to work its will, the Soviet Union chose to eliminate Amin and take over military control of Afghanistan. This decision came at the end of long involvement in the country, which intensified greatly after Marxists seized power in Kabul in 1978. The record suggests that the Kremlin had aimed at getting control over Afghanistan, but found it difficult to control its own Afghan protégés. The result was a rupture with Khalq and the costly and dangerous decision to invade. The invasion left its Parcham clients with the extremely difficult tasks of picking up the threads of government and winning at least the acquiescence of the people. Events since the invasion clearly suggest that it raised more problems for the Soviets and their Afghan allies than it solved.

Early in December 1979 American intelligence sources began to pick up evidence that Russian troops were massing on the northern bank of the Amu Darya (Oxus) River, the boundary between the Soviet Union and Afghanistan. As the Soviet build-up continued, diplomatic notes were sent to Moscow warning of unspecified consequences should the USSR invade Afghanistan. The movement of nearly 100,000 Soviet troops began on December 25. The Soviets' foresight now paid off. The heavy-duty bridges and roadbeds built with their aid allowed their mechanized divisions to rumble southward. Within four days they controlled all major cities.[1]

The invasion appears to have been under serious consideration for several months. Soviet logistical arrangements suggest that they had decided to replace President Amin through military force not long after Taraki died. Their public justification for the intervention was a transparent fabrication. Until his death Amin had led the Khalq government with Soviet support. The Soviets continue to claim that Amin's government asked for more military assistance and they merely obliged. As a good neighbor they threw a lifeline to a government that enjoyed wide diplomatic recognition, including that of the United States, its Western allies, the Muslim nations, and the Third World. Amin's personally hand-picked colleagues on Khalq's Revolutionary Central Committee, the Soviets assert, arrested and executed him for treason and elected in his place his archrival, Babrak Karmal, who had been living in Eastern Europe since the Khalq government accused him of treason in 1978. The Soviet Union claims it rushed in its troops as a response to the committee's call for help.[2] According to this account, there was no break in the continuity of the Marxist leadership in Kabul, only an orderly change at the top of the party. Why, then, was Soviet military help needed? According to the USSR, rebel forces supported by China, Pakistan, Saudi Arabia, and the United States threatened the survival of the Kabul government. Soviet assistance was sought to stop outside intervention and to stabilize the political situation in the country.[3]

Amin was murdered, probably by the Russians, after he refused to agree to an expansion of the Soviet military presence. His death removed the last obstacle to complete Soviet control of the Afghan government. To guarantee this control, an army capable of seizing Kabul and the other major cities had been sent in. The invasion force was not intended to carry the brunt of the fighting against the resistance forces. It was launched to rescue a Marxist government in Kabul from almost certain collapse and from an errant leader who had the presumption to defy Moscow.

In refusing to let the Afghan Marxist regime go under, the Soviet Union extended the Brezhnev Doctrine to Asia. The charges that the United States, China, Pakistan, and Saudi Arabia were combining to destroy the Marxist regime in Kabul were intended to obscure this pivotal change in Soviet behavior. No significant aid had been given the Afghan resistance movement by any country, nor had the resisters planned to seize Kabul with foreign support, as the Soviets and their Parcham allies have alleged. Events since the invasion suggest that the Soviets took their own propaganda too seriously. They seriously miscalculated the amount of force necessary to pacify Afghanistan. By the summer of 1980, the Soviet Union faced the prospect of being bogged down indefinitely in a costly and difficult war.

The invasion represented the first Soviet attempt to annex an Asian state since Mongolia was made a satellite in 1925. As a nation, Afghanistan had never before been conquered. While it had been invaded, its monarchy had functioned independently several times longer than the governments of many modern European countries and those of almost all nations of Asia, Africa, and Latin America. The British invasions of 1839 and 1879 provide a fascinating comparison between nineteenth-century imperialism and contemporary Soviet expansionism. Each time the British attempted to set up a friendly government in Kabul, they lost control over it. This time Afghans are confronted by an invader so massively powerful and technologically superior that the results may be different. Events immediately following the Soviet invasion strongly suggest that a new type of imperialism is being attempted. The USSR's willingness to accept the stigma of armed aggression against a Third World country that posed no threat to it has made the invasion a pivotal move in post–cold-war international politics.

The Soviet bloc argues that the invasion introduced no change in the international situation. The Khalq government had been thoroughly dependent on Soviet support for more than a year and the USSR had already been deeply involved militarily. According to this argument, the change represented by the introduction of almost 100,000 troops in addition to the 10,000 military personnel the Soviets had previously sent was a matter of degree, not of kind. The argument ignores the fact that by overwhelming the Kabul government with a military force far larger than its own, the Soviets effectively took over the struggle for the country. The change was fundamental, not incremental. The situation was altered totally. Even though the Afghan Marxists had depended on the USSR for material and diplomatic support from the beginning, they had seized power on their own behalf. The Soviet invasion came as a result of Khalq's failure to maintain control. The invasion was a unilateral attempt to use force to change the course of a civil war, and it transformed the situation. A beleaguered regime that had been capable of seizing power but was losing its grip was replaced by a puppet government installed by a Soviet expeditionary force. Until December 27, 1979, the Soviet Union had the option of withdrawing without risking a catastrophic defeat. By invading, it had given up that option; now the Soviets had no politically acceptable alternative but to impose their will on the Afghan people.

The chain of events that brought about this crisis at the end of the 1970s is the product of developments that began in the early 1950s. Earlier Afghan-Soviet relations had hovered between distrust and hostility. The amity achieved with Amanullah was a partial exception. Once the Bolsheviks had established themselves in Central Asia, their relationship with the Afghans regressed to mutual aversion, contempt, and fear. The already wide cultural and ideological gulf between them grew ominously as the Bolsheviks incorporated the Muslim peoples of Central Asia into their political and social system. The resulting hostility dominated the relationship throughout the long period of Stalin's rule.

Stalin's death in 1953 came at a critical time for Afghanistan's internal politics. Muhammad Daoud's appointment as prime minister marked the rise of a new generation to power. His plans for fundamental economic and social change required massive help and careful preparations to control the kingdom's recalcitrant peoples. Daoud sought to fulfill both needs by giving the Soviet Union a prominent role in military and economic affairs. The strategy was developed after it became clear that neither the United States nor any other major power could or would match the USSR's involvement in Afghanistan. The Soviet influence was predominant but not intimidating until 1978. Zahir Shah was able to introduce liberal reforms that were drafted and implemented by Western-oriented officials almost all of whom wanted to minimize Soviet influence. Still the USSR continued its military and economic support. The precarious balance between internal self-rule and outside influence shifted once again when Daoud returned to power with Marxist assistance in 1973. The alacrity with which the Soviets moved to assert their influence in Daoud's republic suggests the degree of resentment they must have felt during the liberal era. Yet once again the dynamics of Afghan politics loosened the Soviets' grip when Daoud expelled his Parcham allies from the government and moved closer to neighboring Muslim states. Despite the influence exercised by the Soviet Union since the mid-1950s, there had been considerable room for the autonomous development of Afghan internal and diplomatic policy.

The USSR's Afghan policy operated on overt and covert tracks. Each approach could be used flexibly, either to bring about an eventual seizure of power or to safeguard Soviet interests. Both tracks involved the provision of assistance. The most overt assistance took the form of military and economic aid to the government. Economic programs involving more than $500 million worth of equipment, services, and credits over twenty-five years were supplemented by vigorous diplomatic activity that kept the Soviet mission in constant personal contact with Afghan leaders. Meanwhile, the covert track involved the identification, motivation, guidance, and support of Afghans who could be expected to develop a Marxist organization committed to the overthrow of the very government the USSR was overtly assisting.

Overt aid ensured Soviet influence in almost all sectors of Kabul's official life. Covert connections were almost entirely limited to the very small but rapidly growing segment of the modern educated class. These tracks of influence overlapped in the armed forces. By providing military training to the officer corps, the Soviets were in a position to expose a generation of strategically placed leaders to the Soviet political system. Later they kept in touch with these officers through advisers attached to the Soviet military mission in Kabul. The careers of these officers were linked to their Soviet mentors; Soviet influence did not require that they be Marxists. Such officers could be expected to work against any move toward an anti-Soviet posture by the Kabul government.

Economic aid was designed to broaden Soviet appeal and influence among the nonmilitary Afghan elite. Few of such assistance programs were intended to benefit directly the impoverished majority of the population. These programs provided the dual benefit of laying a foundation for economic progress and creating the logistical means of getting physical control of the country. This two-sided function was most obviously played by the roads, airfields, and communication networks built with Soviet aid. Economic assistance programs also provided the bonus of bringing the Soviets into close personal contact with almost all major agencies of government. Linkage remained weak only in the educational field.

The success of the Soviet assistance programs appeared to offer the strongest assurance that their ambitions did not encompass political control. With things going so well between the two governments at relatively little cost to the Soviets, why should they ever want to disturb the relationship? Yet simultaneously they were helping a semiclandestine Marxist movement to undermine the Afghan political system. Progress along this covert track accelerated when the liberal reforms introduced under Zahir Shah provided opportunities for political activity without serious government harassment. When Daoud was prime minister (1953–63), left-wing radicals were frequently jailed. The liberal policies of the 1960s freed them to build their radical movement. When Daoud returned to power in 1973, the covert and overt tracks met in his own cabinet, where Parcham was strongly represented and a new wave of Soviet economic aid was welcomed. Daoud's attempts to weaken the grip of his Soviet benefactors and his Afghan Marxist allies alienated both.

The role played by the Soviets in the coup of April 27–28, 1978, cannot yet be documented. Soviet resentment at Daoud's improving relations with Pakistan and Iran could not have been lost on the Afghan Marxists. This resentment may have provided sufficient incentive to activate plans for a coup. The Soviets are likely to have known of such plans, but they may not have been in a position to start or to stop them. Critical for an understanding of the Soviet role was the predominance of the Khalq faction in the actual seizure of power. Soviet contacts were closest to the Parcham faction, which appears to have played a lesser, even a passive role in the coup. The prominence of Khalq's role suggests that there was little or no direct Soviet involvement in the coup or in its timing. On April 28, 1978, the Soviets were therefore confronted with the need to come to terms with a Marxist regime in Afghanistan dominated by leaders who owed them little but who suddenly needed their immediate political and material support in order to survive. The result of the Soviet Union's two-track penetration was the coming to power of a Marxist leadership that was ideologically derived from Moscow but whose leaders owed it nothing for the power they had grabbed. After more than two decades of investment, the Soviets had not achieved control; instead they were ensnared in a political alliance with Khalq's reckless leadership.

The Soviet government quickly provided the support Khalq needed. Within its first weeks the Soviet presence was expanded to offset the government's perilously narrow popular support and to offer guidance for its policies. Even so, the Soviets were not able to gain control over events, as the purging of Parcham within three months of the coup demonstrated. The purge soured relations and contributed to the disagreement over Khalq's reform program which surfaced early in 1979. Parcham and the Soviets had argued for slow change and moderation, but the Taraki/Amin government insisted on sudden, drastic change. The Soviet mission in Kabul repeatedly warned the regime of the dangers involved, but was ignored until popular resistance threatened to get out of control. At least for the short term, the Soviets appear to have directed their efforts more at gaining economic and geopolitical benefits for themselves than at giving Afghans the presumed benefits of a socialist society. In doing so, they could plausibly argue that the Khalq regime was not capable of carrying out radical change.

The Soviet government attempted to solve its dilemma by eliminating the increasingly powerful Amin. Its first move was to encourage Taraki to remove Amin in September 1979. When this move failed and Amin was in effective control of the Kabul government, the Soviets were confronted by a client who knew that his greatest danger came from his erstwhile friends. Throughout the autumn Amin and the Soviet mission in Kabul jockeyed for control over the army and what was left of the civil administration. Meanwhile the two sides maintained their uneasy partnership in the attempt to suppress the Afghan resistance.

In early December the Soviets made a last effort to work with Amin—or so it appeared. General Viktor S. Paputin attempted to negotiate a common strategy. The Soviets were convinced by this time that only large Soviet reinforcements of the faltering Afghan army could preserve the Khalq government. Certain of their desire to get rid of him, Amin interpreted their offer to bring in Soviet combat units as a trap; once in Afghanistan, they could be used to remove him. Diplomatic observers differ on what happened between Paputin and Amin. All agree that negotiations broke down, violently.

The Soviet decision to intervene militarily to remove Amin and impose a new Marxist government was one of four choices they were in a position to consider late in 1979. The other three were (1) to continue support of Amin while encouraging Marxist dissidents to use the Afghan armed forces to replace him with a Marxist acceptable to Moscow; (2) to let Amin fall by withdrawing support and then to seek a nonaligned Afghan coalition government willing to have friendly relations with Moscow; (3) to liquidate Amin by military force and then invite moderate resistance leaders to form a nonaligned government that would include Parcham Marxists as the Soviets withdrew their troops.

All of these options had the great advantage of not foisting a puppet government on Afghanistan by military force. Each had serious drawbacks. Amin might have been too clever to permit the first alternative to succeed. The cooperation from moderate resistance leaders required by the second and third alternatives might never have developed or might have come too late. Yet in refusing to attempt one of these alternatives, the Soviets virtually guaranteed all-out popular opposition to the government they tried to impose.

In opting for military intervention without attempting to establish a viable political alternative, the Soviet government made a choice whose costs reach far beyond the casualties and the expenses of mounting a large expedition to control a difficult country. Soviet manpower will be strained if resistance is prolonged and requires the deployment of a force several times the 100,000 committed to the initial invasion. With its long border to secure, the USSR cannot afford to concentrate large forces over a long period in one comparatively small sector. The demands of maintaining dominance in Eastern Europe and of containing the increasingly dangerous Chinese place heavy and constant pressure on Soviet resources.

Even more costly is the price incurred by the spectacle of the crushing of a free people. The struggle waged by the Afghan resistance can be identified with the Third World demand for autonomy from the superpowers. It can also be linked to the increasingly fervent urge of the Muslim world to reclaim its historic role in global affairs. The invasion was an affront to the sensibilities of the nearly one hundred countries that have gained political independence only in the last generation. The Soviet Union has violated a nation that never totally lost its independence even at the crest of European imperialism. In doing so it has risked exposing itself as the new imperialist power in a particularly crude way.

Soviet actions suggest that the final decision to intervene in force came abruptly. Committed to a Marxist regime of some form, the Soviets acted within a narrow policy perspective. Since they were already giving aid, they could see an invasion merely as an extension of their established "friendship policy." Moreover, their objectives in carrying out the invasion appear to have

115

been limited. They could hardly have been unaware of the prospects of expanding their influence in South Asia and the Persian Gulf through a show of force in Afghanistan. The abruptness of their action, however, suggests that they moved to solve the immediate problem in the foreground, the weakness of the Kabul regime. Whatever benefits might be gained through control of Afghanistan could obviously be exploited later. In the meantime there were Afghan insurgents to suppress and a world reaction to finesse.

In reaching its decision to invade Afghanistan, the Soviet leadership had good reason to believe that the time was ripe. The risks attending military intervention in the Middle East were fortuitously low. Iran's seizure of American hostages on November 4, the continuing Muslim resentment over the status of the Palestinians, and the West's growing dependence on Middle Eastern oil had sharply reduced Western influence throughout the region.

Moreover, deteriorating relations with the United States had lessened Soviet interest in maintaining détente. Opposition to the SALT II agreements in the U.S. Sentate cast doubt on the American commitment to a policy of accommodation. This doubt was aggravated by the political opportunism demonstrated in the Senate debate over the issue of the Soviet military presence in Cuba, of which the U.S. government had been aware for years. In Soviet eyes U.S. opportunism was further demonstrated by NATO's announcement that strategic arms based in Western Europe would be increased. These developments, together with the growing rapprochement between the United States and the People's Republic of China, could not have given the Kremlin comfort.

Such circumstances made the decision to invade easier to reach. The circumstances also fitted the pattern of previous Soviet initiatives in Africa and the southern fringe of the Middle East. After seeing their influence dwindle among the oil-exporting nations of the Middle East following their expulsion from Egypt by Anwar Sadat, the Soviets had spread a wide diplomatic, economic, and military net in a "southern strategy."

This strategy encompassed a deep involvement with the Marxists who won control of Angola and Mozambique in 1976. Earlier a close relationship with Somalia permitted the Russians to use naval facilities at the port of Barbera, near the entrance to the Red Sea. By 1978 this arrangement had been canceled out by a more ambitious Soviet attempt to intervene in the revolutionary struggle in Ethiopia. In committing themselves to help the Ethiopian Marxists to recapture the Ogaden, a region held by Somalia, the Soviets lost the friendship and the port facilities of the Somalis. The Soviets' Ethiopian connection brought them into conflict with Muslim nations that had been providing moral and some material support to the long-standing effort of Muslim Eritrea to disengage itself from Christian Ethiopia. Particularly concerned with Eritrean separatism were Saudi Arabia, Sudan, and the royal regime of North Yemen. These Soviet efforts in Africa had been carried through largely by the use of Cuban troops. Such moves may have won the resentment of the offended African and Muslim governments, but it was partially offset by consistent Soviet opposition to the white settler governments of Rhodesia and South Africa.

In the Middle East the Soviets developed intimate military and diplomatic relations with the Marxist government of South Yemen. This Soviet toehold on the Arabian Peninsula offered prospects of penetrating nearby regimes, particularly North Yemen and the lightly populated sultanate of Oman, which commands the mouth of the Persian Gulf. The Soviet Union helped South Yemen to intervene in Oman's Dhofar rebellion in the early 1970s and in its 1979 attack on North Yemen. Such aggressions underlined the Marxist threat to the region. These Soviet moves have alarmed Saudi Arabia's royal family, whose political vulnerability was dramatically demonstrated by the seizure of the Grand Mosque of Mecca in late 1979.

These gains and possible opportunities have been partly balanced by the loss of Soviet influence in the Baathist governments of Syria and Iraq. These Arab socialist regimes were receptive to Soviet military aid and ideological influence, but by 1979 their nationalist proclivities outweighed their gratitude to the Kremlin. A series of internal purges and realignments in the leadership of both countries had notably weakened the positions of those groups closest to the Soviets. At the end of the 1970s the Soviet southern strategy had been far from uniformly successful.

Another factor that could have influenced the decision to invade Afghanistan is the anticipated end of Soviet self-sufficiency in petroleum in the mid-1980s. Control of Afghanistan would ensure a continuing supply of cheap natural gas. But more significant would be the implications in regard to political developments in the Persian Gulf states, especially Iran. The spectacle of the crushing of a stubborn, conservative Muslim people in Afghanistan would strengthen Soviet influence. Though Muslim nations could be expected to resent such Soviet aggression, they might be led to adopt policies of appeasement in order to avoid a similar fate. This threat could be made particularly real through the manipulation of nationalist claims by such minority peoples as the Turkomans, Azerbaijan Turks, Kurds, and Baluch in Iran and by the Pushtuns and Baluch in Pakistan. Success in Afghanistan offered the Soviet government a tool with which to pry concessions out of its neighbors. In the growing competition for Middle East oil, Afghanistan was an obvious stepping-stone toward interference in and perhaps control of the petroleum market.

Given all of these factors, the Soviet decision to invade has inevitably had a grave effect on global and regional affairs. One of these effects has been the return of Afghanistan, after several centuries of obscurity, to the cockpit of the struggle for Eurasian hegemony, a position it had frequently occupied before the modern era of interocean trade and empire.

The Parcham Regime

With the announcement of Amin's death, Tass, the Soviet news agency, quoted Babrak Karmal, the newly elected president and prime minister of the Democratic Republic of Afghanistan (DRA), as follows: "Today is the breaking of the machine of torture of Amin and his henchmen, wild butchers, usurpers and murderers of tens of thousands of our countrymen, fathers, mothers, brothers, sisters, sons and daughters, children and old people."[4]

The declaration set the tone and style of the new regime. Aside from the backing of the Soviet army, it began with two assets only, popular hatred of Amin and the loyalty of a rump of Kabul's educated radicals, perhaps 3,000 followers in all. It strained to get as much mileage as possible out of the feeling against Amin. In consistently bombastic language he was accused of depravity, treachery (especially toward his mentor, Taraki, who was not lionized in death), megalomania, and treason. Among Karmal's first official statements were claims that Amin was an agent of the United States.[5] This charge has been developed with great vigor. Thus both Amin and the insurgents who fought against him are tied to an imperialist and reactionary conspiracy to take over Afghanistan.

Such attempts at vilification have been the Parcham regime's most notable activities. Otherwise it has shown little ability to live up to the role that the Soviet government has assigned to it. It has been paralyzed by vicious feuds among its leaders; it has been forced to rely on Soviet and Eastern European advisers to carry out the most routine functions of government; its armed forces have disintegrated and some of its best remaining units have attempted to revolt; it has not been able to keep the peace even in its capital city, where Marxist factions ambush each other; and it has virtually no constructive contact with the 90 percent of the population that lives in the countryside.

Its failures have greatly complicated the Soviets' task. The achievement of stable control required that Parcham attract some degree of national support. But what worked in Hungary and Czechoslovakia has produced a quagmire in Afghanistan. The process that installed Parcham tarnished, probably irrevocably, its pretensions to legitimacy and popularity. Karmal arrived in Kabul (via a Soviet transport plane) only after Amin had been killed.[6] His first pronouncements were broadcast by Soviet Radio from Tashkent on the Kabul Radio frequency.[7]

These humiliations were compounded once the Soviets were established. Karmal was forced to accept several leaders of the Khalq faction as his colleagues in the new government. Asadullah Sarwari, installed as deputy prime minister, had served as Taraki's secret police chief and had fallen out with Amin. Muhammad Ismail Danish, the new minister of mines and industries, was a holdover from Amin's final cabinet, as were Dastagir Panjshiri and Saleh Muhammad Zeari, both named to the new party central committee. Another Khalqi, Sayyid Muhammad Gulabzoi, was named minister of the interior, with authority over internal security. Several of these Khalq survivors soon demonstrated that they were not reconciled to Karmal's leadership. Scorned by most of his countrymen as a puppet of the Russians, Karmal continued in the Afghan Marxist tradition as a leader who could not trust his closest colleagues.

The government's impotence was further displayed by the obvious control exercised by Russian "advisers" in ministries and agencies. When they arrived in force, the Soviets found that two years of purges, arrests, and intimidation had brought about the virtual collapse of government. Few of the surviving Parchamists were qualified to staff top agencies and ministry divisions. The reliability of nonpolitical officials was uncertain. The situation offered an excellent opportunity to clean house, and the Soviets took advantage of it by staffing the Afghan government more thoroughly than any other state in the Soviet bloc, with the possible exception of Mongolia. Soviet advisers now set ministry policy and Soviet lieutenants carried it out. Afghan officials became ornaments, handing the phone to their Soviet counterparts when matters of substance were to be discussed.[8] The few Russian-speaking Afghans were at a premium for middle- and upper-level government assignments. Once again, earlier development assistance paid off. A new wave of civilian advisers took over a section of the Microyan, an apartment complex built by the Soviets supposedly for modernized Afghan families. From the operation of the utilities to the control of the state, Soviet influence became total. The Parcham leaders were left with the ugly jobs of flushing out and punishing opponents and creating a facade of self-rule that might convince the outside world of its legitimacy as a sovereign government.

The Karmal government announced policies to broaden its popular acceptance and to build a new foundation for its authority. It tried to generate some popularity by including non-Marxists at the top of government, by freeing the political prisoners held by Amin, by revoking or delaying the radical reforms imposed by Khalq, by promising to protect private property and individual rights, and by demonstrating respect for and acceptance of Islam. The new government planned to build its authority on a foundation of a strengthened army and militia, effective educational indoctrination, and a start toward heavy industrialization with liberal Soviet help. This would have been an ambitious agenda for any government. For one that was torn by internal dissension and distrust, threatened by armed revolt, not permitted to run its own affairs, and despised by its protectors, its objectives seemed unrealistic. As its plans became frustrated, the Parcham government resorted to broadcasting propaganda in order to establish its presence internally and its bona fides internationally.

Much of Parcham's difficulty in taking hold as an effective government was due to the failure of the Soviet plan to pacify the country quickly, as we shall see in Chapter 7. Parcham's isolation from the population has severely restricted its operations. Almost as damaging has been the rancor among its leaders. The mix of politicians, Khalq as well as Parcham, and soldiers with whom the Soviets forced Karmal to work was unstable at best.

Dominating the internal politics of the regime is its need to base its legitimacy on the coup of April 27, 1978. The regime claims it has inherited a revolution that was perverted and then betrayed by Amin. This argument allows it to ignore the Soviet invasion and to base its right to rule on an Afghan-made coup. Accordingly, Afghan Marxists who had opposed or later repudiated Amin are legitimate participants in the revolution, eligible to serve in its government. Making a virtue of necessity, Karmal accepted old Khalq rivals in his government.[9]

This reunion has been a heavy burden. Such Khalq stalwarts as Asadullah Sarwari and Gulabzoi, standing fast in their support of radical social change, insisted on keeping Khalq's red flag, opposed non-Marxists in the government, and refused to accommodate capitalist trade or Islamic sentiment. More immediately dangerous were the enmities left from earlier power struggles. Some Parchamists had suffered painfully from the purges and imprisonments imposed by the Khalq faction under Taraki and Amin. Sarwari, as head of the secret police under Taraki, is alleged to have personally tortured Asadullah Keshtmand, Karmal's second deputy prime minister. The desire for vengeance underlay the charged atmosphere. The tensions gave rise to a flood of rumors. In late February 1980 an argument in the cabinet led to stories that Sarwari had seriously wounded Keshtmand in a shootout, and that Karmal's brother, Mahmud Baryalay, had been killed. Keshtmand was evacuated to the Soviet Union. Baryalay immediately turned up very much alive, but on Soviet, not Afghan, television. A few days earlier there were rumors that Karmal himself had been deposed by opponents in the government.

These rumbles of internal rivalry increased in March and April as the government strove to establish its revolutionary line in time for the April 27 anniversary celebration. The Khalq hard-liners continued their opposition to a new flag, a united-front strategy, and the indefinite presence of the Russians in the country. There was much jockeying for the various ministries. *The Economist* of London reported that Gulabzoi purged most of the senior officials of the Interior Ministry by locking them out of their offices.[10]

The struggle between Khalqis and Parchamists was complicated by the role of prominent military officers in the government. The most important of these officers were the revolutionary heroes Major General Abdul Qadir, now a member of the Revolutionary Council's presidium, and Colonel Muhammad Aslam Watanjar, serving both on the council and as minister of communications. Watanjar and Colonel Sherjan Mazduryar, now minister of transport, had maneuvered between the Khalq and Parcham factions before falling out with Amin in September 1979. They survived under the protection of the Russians. These military officers had their resentments and their Soviet connections. Qadir reportedly had been tortured under Taraki and was scheduled for execution until his sentence was commuted by Amin. As pressures built up in the Karmal government, these political soldiers were forced to take sides. Internal factionalism produced a crisis in July 1980. By threatening to resign, Karmal apparently forced the Soviets to back him in a purge of his rivals. Watanjar had reportedly already left for the Soviet Union. *The Economist* reports that Sarwari was sent under Soviet protection as ambassador to Mongolia, a neat reversal of what happened to Karmal two years earlier. Clipping Gulabzoi's wings, Karmal took away his control over local officials in the Ministry of the Interior. Karmal then moved to replace Khalq army commanders with loyal Parchamists. This move led to the mutinies of the Fourteenth Armored Division at Ghazni and the Puli Charkhi garrison in mid-July.[11] With Soviet backing, Karmal should win his bid to take full control of the government, but at the cost of a further narrowing of its political and military base.

An attempt to broaden the government's appeal was made in January 1980, when three non-Marxists were given cabinet appointments: Muhammad Ibrahim Azim in Public Health, Fazal Rahim Mohmand in Agriculture, and Muhammad Khan Jalalar (who had served in Daoud's cabinet) in Commerce. These appointments were part of a united-front strategy favored by the Soviets and Karmal.[12] A further demonstration of accommodation of non-Marxists was the announcement of the appointment of two cabinet advisers who had been outstanding progressive leaders during the liberal constitutional period of the 1960s: Rawan Farhadi and Muhammad Siddiq Farhang. Farhadi had served as secretary to the cabinet throughout the constitutional period; Farhang had served on the committee that drafted the 1964 constitution. These appear to be figurehead appointments; there is no evidence that either of these men is in a position to influence the government. It is possible that these appointments were announced without their consent. While Karmal struggled with personnel problems, his central task was that of creating a new social policy. Abrupt radical change was rejected; reconciliation was offered. Afghan society was declared to be in a transitional stage suited to a united-front leadership. In his initial speech President Karmal promised:

> . . . the Government of the Democratic Republic of Afghanistan is established on a national united front under the leadership of the working class and all the toilers of Afghanistan. . . . While under the circumstances it is *not our direct duty to practice socialism,* the new government deems it its historic national duty to . . . perform the following urgent duties:
> (1) Proclaim the release of all political prisoners . . .
> (2) Abolish all anti-democratic and anti-human regulations and all arrests, arbitrary persecutions, house searches and inquisitions.
> (3) Respect the sacred principles of Islam . . . , protect family unity and observe legal and lawful private ownership . . .
> (4) Revive . . . revolutionary tranquility, peace and order in the country.
> (5) Insure . . . conditions conducive to democratic freedoms such as the freedom to form progressive and patriotic parties . . .
> (6) Pay serious attention to our youth.[13]

Such measures were intended to create popular acceptance of what the regime continued to call the "New Model Revolution." The problem was to make these measures work despite the government's internal divisions, its weakness, and the turmoil that had been unleashed by the revolution and the invasion. Thousands of prisoners were released in early January in a gesture intended to dramatize the difference between the Karmal and Amin regimes. Directives were issued banning arbitrary arrests and imprisonments; representatives of the International Red Cross were invited to check the condition and status of prisoners (they found fifty-seven political prisoners still being held). But Kabul's citizens remained convinced that they were subject to sudden seizure, disappearance, and torture. In the aftermath of bloody demonstrations in the capital and other cities in late February, these fears were realized. With its authority under constant challenge, the regime employed summary measures to maintain order.

Beginnings and gestures were made to reassure religious leaders and capitalists, particularly traders with profitable export businesses, that their roles would be respected in the transitional order. Government proclamations began in the name of Allah, the Islamic green was restored to the national flag, Karmal kissed and hugged mullahs on television. Permits to conduct foreign trade were to be made available to merchants. The objectionable land and marriage regulations were no longer enforced.

On the second anniversary of the 1978 coup, Parcham announced the "Fundamental Principles of the Democratic Republic of Afghanistan," which provided a format for rule by Parcham as an elite, vanguard party (the PDPA) acting through the government. The period since the Soviet invasion was referred to as the "second phase" of the "revolution." The party formally took upon itself all powers of government. The party is to go through the motions of calling a national loya jirgah to ratify a constitution to be drafted by the party's revolutionary council.

The Fundamental Principles do not describe the government's program as socialist, but they reduce the roles and autonomy left to non-Marxist institutions. All facets of society are declared to be subject to revolutionary change and the party's authority. Reconciliation thus becomes a matter of gaining popular acquiescence through redistributive reforms, economic development, and cultural/educational conditioning. Although it had made no real progress in any of these directions, the Parcham government insisted that it was prepared to embark on a new era.

While Parcham was attempting to establish its revolutionary direction, it also moved to strengthen its grip on the armed forces and the educational system. Reinforced by Soviet declarations of new assistance, it also announced new economic development programs.

In March, after the army had dwindled to less than half its pre-invasion strength, a new conscription law was issued, extending indefinitely the service terms of new and old recruits alike. In an attempt to improve conditions for soldiers, their notoriously low pay was increased and they were issued more stylish uniforms. Much attention to the "glory" and "courage" of the army was paid in the government news media as high school graduates were "invited" to "volunteer" for duty. Meanwhile government impressment gangs were reportedly searching the cities for draftees who had failed to report.

The collapse of much of the army and the shortcomings of the undisciplined party militia as a fighting force limited the credibility of the government's claims of autonomy. With regard to military manpower it faced a vicious circle. Having no control over most of the rural population, it had to conscript men mostly from the cities. The drafting of city youth added further to the resentment that produced urban uprisings. Positive inducements to serve palled alongside the dangers of pacification duty and the open contempt of the Russian forces. As a result, draftees were hard to find and tended to be unenthusiastic recruits when they were inducted. Under these circumstances, the prospects for strengthening Parcham's military arm remained bleak.

Education offered a more fundamental and long-term antidote for the government's weakness. Plans were continued to build a national school system on the Soviet model: ten years of compulsory education followed by a broad range of technical and professional or academic higher education for the gifted. The new regime continued Khalq's promise to provide higher education to all secondary school graduates who wanted it. While plans went ahead to make the study of Russian compulsory in secondary and higher study, minorities were to be recognized as part of the national culture by the introduction of their languages into the school curriculum.

Parcham found progress toward these goals extremely difficult. In many parts of the country schools had been closed, often because they had been destroyed by the resistance. Schoolteachers, considered to be agents of Marxist indoctrination, were favorite targets for assassination unless they joined the resistance. The situation in the cities appeared to be more promising for the government, but by April urban schools were disrupted by factional disputes between Marxist teachers and students. Students opposed to the regime began to stage demonstrations. Within four months of its installation the Parcham government was attempting to run an educational system that was rapidly becoming nonexistent in the countryside and in pandemonium in the cities. Similar frustrations were experienced in attempts to revive the economy. Foreign trade and internal development projects had been paralyzed by the near chaos of the last months of the Khalq regime. There were few opportunities to move from planning proposals to concrete projects. Harvests and crop distribution were seriously disrupted by the fighting. It was impossible to provide adequate security for Soviet advisers at industrial and agricultural project sites. For example, it was reported in May that Russian textile advisers had to be evacuated from mills at Baghlan, Herat, and Kandahar.[14] Other bilateral and internationally assisted programs also came to a standstill, partly because of the dangers to foreigners, partly because of transportation blockages and diplomatic impasses. As a result, the Parcham regime and its Soviet advisers had little chance to restore the economy to its pre-1979 state, much less to embark on new developments. The cities suffered sudden shortages in cereals, vegetable oils, and tea, and, of course, sharply rising prices. Urban economic distress undermined the scant acceptance the regime had achieved.

In the countryside, cultivating and harvesting had to compete with guerrilla campaigning and Soviet scorched-earth tactics. The result was pockets of famine in the most contested areas and glut in regions whose harvests could not get to market. Crop production declined as much as 25 percent nationally, according to some reports.

Given its Marxist ideology and the circumstances in which it was thrust into power, the Parcham government's failure to win acceptance, to address the country's chronic problems, and even to organize itself effectively was probably unavoidable. This failure has made Soviet control of the country all the more transparent, adding greatly to problems of pacification and drawing international opposition to the invasion and subsequent occupation. So far the Soviets have used the straightforward tactic of running all important affairs, leaving Parcham as a pathetic facade, unrecognized by most Muslim nations and despised by the Afghans. Unless and until the Soviet forces physically subdue the Afghan freedom fighters, Parcham's prospects will remain dim.

7

The Struggle
for Afghanistan

Despite their overwhelming military strength, the Soviet
forces have not been able to conquer Afghanistan. The cities,
the main roads, the air bases were seized in a matter of days.
Since then a modern, mechanized army of more than 100,000
has made little progress in reducing insurgent control over the
countryside, while its hold over the cities and the roads has been
increasingly challenged.

The only permanent achievement of the invasion has been the
elimination of Amin. The Soviets badly miscalculated the impact
of his murder. Instead of cheering the Soviets for delivering
them from a monster, the people rose against them as invaders.
The Parcham government has been too unpopular, divided, and
inept to help the Russians to pacify the population or to provide
the basis for permanent Soviet domination. In fact, the government led by Karmal has been a crippling liability to the Soviet
forces. Its dependence on the Russians for survival evokes
hatred from all sections of the population except for the fewer
than 5,000 Marxists and political opportunists who continue to
serve it. Mass revulsion against it has spread to the Afghan army,
which has melted to one-third of its former size as a result of
purges, mutinies, desertions, and battle casualties.

Parcham's weakness has been a serious disappointment to the
Soviet command. Equally significant has been Russian miscal-
culation of the effectiveness and tenacity of the resistance. The
almost total uselessness of the Afghan army against insurgents

129

in the countryside has forced the Soviets to use their own troops in search-and-destroy missions. They have found that shock tactics based on massive air and armored firepower can hurt and scatter the guerrilla groups, but not destroy them. The difficult terrain and the fighting qualities of the mujahidin make it evident that pacification will require a much larger force than the Soviet government has thus far deployed.

World reactions during the first six months after the invasion did not materially affect Soviet policy. The diplomatic costs were acceptable. Soviet behavior has been determined by the ferocity and universality of the resistance. The resulting struggle threatens to engulf Soviets and Afghans in an orgy of unlimited violence.

Reports of the fighting, both from the press and from official agencies, have inevitably given a distorted picture. Except for a brief period in January 1980, noncommunist journalists have been denied entry. Since then direct reporting has been limited to the few daring and resourceful journalists who have posed as tourists or have accompanied resistance groups operating in the rural areas. Their authentic but necessarily fragmentary accounts fill a few of the many gaps left by the stream of propaganda produced by all sides. Descriptions of battles and incidents issued by the resistance organizations headquartered in Pakistan have been published in the Pakistani and Indian press and occasionally repeated in the Western press. Such reports, designed to promote the cause of each resistance group and to attract international support, frequently exaggerate resistance exploits, especially Soviet casualties. When their own guerrillas are involved, their reports can be trusted on the location and intensity of the fighting, though they tend to ignore defeats and offer little information on the activities of resistance groups that have poor outside connections—the Hazaras, the Nuristanis, most of the Uzbeks and Turkomans in the north, and groups fighting in the Herat and Farah regions of western Afghanistan.

Broadcasts by Radio Kabul are similarly one-sided. They tend to downplay resistance activities and to disguise unrest in the cities. Their constant calls on the people to rally against foreign provocateurs and rebels duped by them are signs of the extent of Parcham's insecurity. The Soviets' reports have been especially uninformative. They refused to admit that resistance was serious until May, characterizing it as banditry or foreign subversion. Outside intelligence assessments of the conflict that have filtered or leaked into the Western and Indian press have been too vague, conflicting, or uncertain to be convincing. Care must be taken in accepting their estimates of Soviet or Afghan troop levels or casualties and their conclusions regarding the effectiveness or prospects of insurgent groups or changes in Soviet pacification strategy. A reliable description of the Soviet-Afghan war awaits its conclusion. There may never be a definitive account. Too much will go undocumented or will be deliberately hidden. Many facts about major episodes will be suppressed. Press reports, despite the limitations we have noted, must necessarily be relied on for most of the evidence; lesser roles are played by personal interviews and correspondence with eyewitnesses.

Initially the invading forces were not directed at the resistance forces spread throughout the countryside. The winter snows in January and February 1980 made movement and armed hostilities difficult for both sides. Only in the isolated provinces of Badakhshan and Takhar did large numbers of Soviet troops immediately become engaged in fighting the mujahidin. The limitations on combat during the winter gave the foreign journalists present in mid-January the impression that the invaders had the country well in hand, that the resistance was overawed by massive modern force. When this proved not to be the case a few weeks later, the credibility even of "neutral" observers suffered.

Tactics

Given its original expectation that Afghan troops would be able to reduce the rural-based resistance to an acceptable level, the Soviet command initially deployed its forces near population centers. Soviet planners believed that once the potentially hostile units of the Afghan army had been disarmed, screened, and then sent out to pacify the countryside, there would be little need for Soviet troops to become heavily engaged in the fighting. Such calculations were evident in the choice of five reserve divisions with limited combat training to form the bulk of the invasion force. They were Tajiks, Uzbeks, and Turkomans drawn almost completely from the USSR's Central Asian republics. Most of these troops could understand Dari or one or more of the northern regional languages. The Soviet command was disappointed to find that Afghans were hostile to these regional cousins. These divisions were officered by European Russians. Some Central Asian informants are reported to have claimed that "all the personnel of a Soviet combat brigade were executed ... for refusing to fight against fellow Muslims in Afghanistan."[1]

Their lack of preparation for the invasion was graphically reported by Robert Fisk of *The Times* of London, who in early January traveled with a division moving south along the highway from Termez, on the Soviet border, to Kabul. The reserve troops that made up the division lacked the training to take cover when they came under sniper fire. Their officers had not been furnished with maps of their route and had not been briefed on the kind of resistance they might face. Such units could have been expected to carry out only relatively passive garrison duties, such as patrolling the cities after curfew.[2]

One elite parachute division, the 105th, had been flown in earlier to seize the critical airports and air bases, to clear the main highways for the infantry divisions, and to crush Afghan units loyal to Amin. It was the one unit capable of the mobile, concentrated firepower necessary to wipe out visible resistance quickly and hence to demonstrate the apparent invincibility of the invasion force. With the logistical and support units brought in to prepare semipermanent fortified camps along the main road loop, Red Army troop strength reached 85,000 within ten days of the invasion.[3]

The Soviets' optimism is clearly implied by their initial choice of units better versed in the local languages than in military tactics. The initial airborne blitzes of key locations followed by a

Turkoman woman, Samangan

massive show of armor—six divisions rolled southward in some 4,500 tanks and armored personnel carriers—were designed to overawe the resistance. Reorganized Afghan units, supported when necessary by Soviet air and armor strikes, were then expected to reduce rural resistance to a minimum.

Within a few weeks the fallacies of such planning were obvious. Soviet troops were taking alarmingly high casualties, even those engaged in garrison duty. The population was not overawed; an unusually severe winter had only delayed its full reaction. Its ferocity was clear from the large number of fatal assaults on Red soldiers. Before January 10 several Soviet soldiers were killed in Kabul by civilians wielding rocks, meat cleavers, or weapons taken away from them.[4] Fifty Russians were reported slaughtered near Mazar-i-Sharif when they were surprised by a mob after being lured to a game of buzkashi, Afghanistan's national sport.[5]

As the snows melted, guerrilla groups became more active. By late February the roads were no more secure than they had been in the last days of Amin. Traffic had to move by convoy, with no guarantee of safe arrival. Travel became particularly hazardous on two of the main highways leading out from Kabul, to the Khyber Pass and to Salang Pass. The Kandahar–Herat highway was also frequently blocked. In March resistance groups began seriously to threaten the previously safe road from Kabul to Kandahar.

Guerrilla roadblocking tactics were simple but effective. The road would be covered by stones dislodged from a cliff, mined, or strewn with disabled vehicles. The stopped traffic would then be sniped at or captured, depending on the strength of the units defending the road. Captured drivers and passengers had various fates. Frequently they were robbed and let go; some, suspected of working for or being associated with the government, were kidnapped or killed. Most civilians, particularly bus passengers, were released and allowed to proceed. Some were forced to join the resistance on pain of being shot for refusing. Such harsh treatment and the hijacking of vehicles and supplies gave the Soviet government a basis for branding freedom fighters in general as "bandits," but the effectiveness of their interruption

The Khyber Pass

of traffic dramatized the failure of the Soviets' attempt to impose control. It has been a major factor in their decision to reconsider their pacification strategy.

The assumptions behind that strategy were brought further into question in February by a wave of strikes and attacks on the government in at least ten cities. Kabul was in turmoil for a week. The uprisings demonstrated that the population, urban as well as rural, was determined to oppose Parcham and the invading Soviets.

The Soviet forces took over administration of the cities in the process of crushing the strikes. Displays of Soviet armored strength were now extended throughout the days and nights. In the Kunar Valley the Soviets lashed out with their first large-scale ground offensive. Toward the end of February two Soviet divisions extended these attacks to adjacent Laghman and Nangarhar provinces. Reliance on Afghan units to pacify the countryside was tacitly given up. They were now used as auxiliaries and sometimes as forward elements, in positions that placed them between insurgent and Soviet guns.

The failure of the Soviet command to find significant Afghan help to pacify the country threatened to aggravate global responses to the invasion. By participating directly in pacification, the Soviets were required to use terror and destruction in order to crush opposition. They have depended heavily on massive firepower in conducting search-and-destroy missions and in carrying out punitive bombing attacks, and have used gas and napalm in reprisals against resisting villages. Bombing, strafing, artillery fire, and machine-gunning from helicopters have led to numerous cases of indiscriminate slaughter. Civilian casualties have been heavy. The number of refugees who have fled to Pakistan and Iran has doubled, and an increasing number of refugees are wandering within Afghanistan itself. Already disrupted by the conflict generated by the Khalq regime, the agricultural cycle has been thrown into further disarray by the flight of labor and breakdowns in transportation and marketing.

Probably the most important advantage that their monopoly of modern military equipment gives the Soviets is their ability to strike without warning with overwhelming force, as they have done in the Pushtun areas—Kunar, Nangarhar, Paktia, and later Ghazni. Soviet jets drop rockets, bombs, and napalm to catch rural populations in their fortress-like mud compounds or in the open countryside. When flushed from their homes or from ground cover, they are gunned down by massive strafing from helicopter gunships or by commando units parachuted into villages immediately after bombing and rocket raids. The combined effect of these tactics was described in an Associated Press report of an attack on Chigha Sarai, in the Kunar Valley, in March:

> When Abdel Wahid fled the Soviet tanks and planes pounding his native Afghan village "everything was burning. Nobody was left to bury the dead."

The farmer was among hundreds of shivering, hungry refugees, most of them women and children in poor condition, who reached safety in Pakistan . . . after a five-day trek through the snow-covered mountains of eastern Afghanistan.

. . . before dawn on March 1 . . . hundreds of Russian tanks suddenly appeared on the hills on all sides and started shelling the village. Jet planes came and dropped bombs. When most of the village was destroyed, they dropped parachute troops from big helicopters and other helicopters landed troops . . . the rebels continued to resist, killing "many of the Russians," but the Soviets then called in planes which "dropped bombs and napalm. . . . Two of my cousins were killed. Many, many others were killed. All the people who could still walk fled into the mountains. The last time I saw the village everything was burning."[6]

Highly mechanized warfare is also intended to keep Soviet casualties low. Hand-to-hand combat has been avoided; Russian troops immediately find themselves at a disadvantage when they leave their vehicles. Guerrilla sniper fire is often deadly. Bullet-proof vests have become standard Soviet issue for combat soldiers.

These tactics also have their disadvantages. Jet pilots have great difficulty maneuvering for targets in the narrow upland valleys. They have been more effective near the main highways, most of which are located in the wider, lower valleys and stretches of desert plain. Columns of tanks and armored personnel carriers maneuvering in the hills are often forced into long files. This deployment provides the guerrillas with opportunities to immobilize them by blocking front and rear vehicles. The deadliness of such tactics has been enhanced by the tendency of Soviet vehicles to break down in the mud or dust that clogs most Afghan roads. Their clumsiness in rough terrain makes Soviet tanks vulnerable to ambushes when they have lost the advantage of surprise.

Achievement of surprise has been rare. The Soviet forces have been poorly prepared to make use of their mobility. Reactions to guerrilla actions in various parts of the country are often too slow to catch the mujahidin in exposed positions. Stuart

Auerbach, writing for the *Washington Post*, quotes a Western source in Kabul: "'[The Soviets] are always slow to respond. Their morning attacks are planned the night before and it sometimes takes a day or two to move against the insurgents. There are no hunting operations of the sort the Americans ran in Vietnam.'" A Western diplomat told him, "'There is an uprising in Badakhshan and they rush up there. Then something happens in Ghazni and they have to race there. They can't seem to mount more than one operation at a time and they never are able to clean up an area. They are just running themselves ragged trying to fight something like the rebels.'"[7]

These observers believe that the Soviet command structure does not give enough authority to officers in the field. Such inflexibility actually turns the lack of coordination among resistance groups into an advantage for them. The randomness of their actions keeps the overly centralized Soviet command constantly off balance.

Such weaknesses of command have not been compensated for by special weapons. Use of antipersonnel gas has not appreciably improved the effectiveness of the pacification effort. Afghan army units are reported to have used gas (under Soviet advisers) before the invasion. Western intelligence analysts quickly identified gas decontamination equipment brought in by Soviet units in early January. Such equipment is standard issue for mechanized divisions. While reports persist that the Russians are using Soman, a nerve gas that could cause large numbers of deaths, most of the available evidence suggests that they are using a highly virulent incapacitating gas—perhaps phosgene oxide. It can be lethal in confined areas: caves, narrow defiles, walled spaces. It has been dropped in canisters from helicopters. Reports of its use have been most frequent in the Badakhshan-Takhar region, where confirmation is virtually impossible to obtain. Refugees from Kunar and Nangarhar also claim it has been used there. One of the most detailed descriptions was provided by *Newsweek*: ". . . the skin of the victims developed brown blotches, swelled and then peeled off. Gassed victims suffered nose bleeds, nausea, severe diarrhea, then paralysis—and death."[8]

Anthony Paul, writing for *Asiaweek*, provided different testimony:

> In interviews with four refugees in as many different [refugee] camps, I was told of a gas dropped in canisters from gunships. The grey canisters were similar to drums with a capacity of about 200 litres of water. When they disintegrated on contact with the ground, a brownish-white smoke or mist emerged, which spread across a battlefield or in an area in which mujahidin were hiding— wooded areas or caves—causing exposed skin to sting unbearably, eyes and noses to run copiously, and breathing to be so constricted as to cause a pain in the chest similar to that suffered during a heart attack. Many victims lost consciousness. If a mujahid or civilian was within about 100 yards of the canister impact point, there was a very strong likelihood of death. Beyond that radius, tribesmen assured me, it was possible to survive a gas attack by breathing through a water-soaked turban or handkerchief wrapped around charcoal.
>
> . . . The gas does not compare, for example, with World War I gas attacks. . . . One measure of its efficacy came in March in Sukhrud village about four miles west of Jalalabad. In an afternoon of attacks on mujahidin trenches on low ground about 200 to 300 metres west of the settlement, Soviet gunships dropped five or six canisters, killing only nineteen adult males and two boys.[9]

Such terror weapons have not brought significant advantages. The Soviets have too few troops to secure the areas decimated by either gas or bombing attacks. Terror and shock tactics have lost some of their impact as the rural population has learned to anticipate them. By themselves, these tactics cannot crush or even markedly diminish resistance. The human costs they inflict guarantee unremitting hostility. Without sufficient manpower and firepower to assault and hold large sections of territory and population, the Soviets have been unable to pacify the country.

By the summer of 1980 the Soviet command appeared to recognize that it had reached an impasse. A highly publicized withdrawal of elements of an armored division was made in June. Although propaganda and diplomacy were the most immediate purposes of the announced withdrawal, it suggests a change in the composition and tactics of the Soviet forces. At virtually the same time, Western diplomats in Kabul noted the arrival of units specially trained for counterinsurgency. The failure to suppress opposition has also forced an examination of the need to protect Soviet world standing as the war goes on. The use of units better equipped for quick thrusts into remote and rugged terrain and for close combat would greatly improve their pacification effort. The extent to which the Soviet command is willing to commit its best troops to Afghanistan and their ability to cope with the conditions and the enemy there remain to be seen.

Afghan mujahid tactics conform to the classic requirements of guerrilla warfare: small group actions using the cover of night, territory remote from centers of power, and a supporting population to inflict damage on an entrenched authority with vastly greater military resources. A great part of the mujahidin's strategy is the dramatization of resistance: making their presence known through assassinations, attacks on outposts and installations, the blocking of roads, sudden appearances in towns and villages to recruit men and collect supplies. In June *Pravda* gave an excellent general description of mujahid tactics:

> . . . the Afghan rebels have reduced the size of their individual fighting units to 30–40 men, and they like to use ambushes at bridges and narrow places. . . . They blow up a bridge or create an avalanche, and then open fire from high terrain. . . . If a strong military column is passing, they let the reconnaissance and advance units through. Then they open fire suddenly and with close aim, and scatter quickly. . . . They mine roads, and then set up rifle and machine-gun cover of the mined area. One can feel the hand of professional foreign instructors.[10]

These techniques have been extended to include the fomenting of strikes in the cities and inducement of Afghan military units to desert and mutiny. Its propaganda value aside, one must wonder how seriously the Soviet authorities take *Pravda*'s remark about foreign instructors. They have turned up precious little evidence of them; the comment reflects an insistence that the Afghan resistance is not capable of developing its own guerrilla tactics. Given the large Russian literature on the history and anthropology of Afghanistan, much of it excellent, it is surprising that the Soviet command did not anticipate effective guerrilla tactics.

Despite their shortage of modern weapons, their divisions and rivalries, and their lack of a tradition of unified action on a national scale, the mujahidin control most of the countryside. In April the *Far Eastern Economic Review* reported that civilian government and party officials had been unable to take up village positions in Baghlan for two months.[11] Few other provinces were safer. In the cities, security collapsed. Hemmed in by stringent police measures—curfews, informers, troop concentrations at street crossings and public buildings—officials and civilians alike had a sense of a situation about to explode. John Shaw, reporting from Kabul, wrote:

> The atmosphere of the city fluctuates between acute tension and chronic fear. In the tea house all heads lift from sipped cups when anyone enters. A slammed door, an auto exhaust backfiring, the passing of a military vehicle, a ringing phone, the clumsy crash of trays or pots in a cafe—any of these sounds turns eyes nervously, stops conversations. People do not loiter in the streets, except at bus stops and around food stores. . . .
>
> Because phones are often tapped, or may be, embassies, missions and the few remaining individual foreigners in Kabul use code words to pass daily signals of the estimated danger level. Some of the phrases, on an ascending scale of warning, are "Phase One," "Phase Two," "Ground Fog," "Fog," "Bad Weather" meaning roughly, take care, stay at home, likely trouble, emergency.[12]

Yet while the mujahidin have made themselves felt everywhere, they have lacked the weapons, the organization, and the cohesion to threaten the Soviet military position seriously. A gallant naiveté persists, well expressed by the young Hizb-i-Islami commander for the region south of Kandahar: "He had not personally encountered the much-feared, heavily armoured MI-24 [helicopter] gunships in action, but if and when he did, he had a plan. 'The Commander says he believes he can get them

The east side of Kabul, from Sher Darwaza Mountain

with large-bore rifles—elephant guns. . . . Also he'll use blunt bullets on them. He will be cutting the ends off his bullets.'"[13]

The commander's confidence in elephant guns might change quickly if Soviet units become as active in his region as they have been in Paktia. Such jauntiness had been common among mujahidin there before the Soviet units struck in force. Afzal Khan, a Pakistani journalist who witnessed a Pushtun attack on an army post in October 1979, found the mujahidin badly prepared to take on modern units:

> They were armed with a collector's assortment of weapons—cudgels, swords, axes, daggers, shotguns and rifles ranging from vintage World War I British Enfields to captured Soviet Kalishnikov automatics. They ranged in age, too, from youths to graybeards, but all of them were crusaders, waging a holy war against the Soviet-backed regime. . . .

The battle began just after 10 p.m. As the guerrillas approached the bunkers on the outskirts of the garrison, the sky blazed with streaking red tracer bullets. Machine guns answered the attackers' rifle fire. Exploding shells from Russian howitzers threw up a haze of dust and smoke. . . . A direct hit killed one guerrilla and wounded eight.

A Molotov cocktail set fire to a government tank. "Allah-o-Akbar!" the attackers cried. . . .

The shouts soon ebbed to whispers. The firing ceased. Expert and thrifty marksmen, Afghan tribesmen usually count on killing one man with one bullet. Since they must buy ammunition for their rifles at $3 a round in Pakistani bazaars, they can scarcely afford the luxury of a second shot. . . .

On the offensive the guerrillas are at [a] . . . disadvantage. They can attack garrisons only at night, when they can't be spotted by planes, helicopters or tanks. Even then, they seldom penetrate the outer perimeters, which are laced with mines. . . .

An attack on Jaji, another government garrison in Paktia . . . , had to be postponed at the last minute because of a shortage of bullets. Two days later . . . an assault on Jaji was finally launched. Hasan Gailani had managed to borrow from the Zadran tribe a tank which, along with a couple of 75-millimeter guns, supported the offensive by about 5,000 mujahids.

But the supply of shells was still limited and the few hits the guerrillas scored were not enough.[14]

Writing several months later, Edward Girardet argued that Pushtun insurgents harassing Jalalabad had neither the means nor the strategy to inflict more than mosquito bites on the Soviet garrison.

Halting in a stony clearing, the commander pointed to the lights and told us that it was a Soviet base. . . . "You must watch from here," whispered the commander. It was apparently too dangerous for us to go any farther because of mine fields. . . .

Leaving two armed rebels with us, the bulk of the group edged forward. Suddenly the mujahideen opened up. Tracers soared through the sky and we could hear the echoing cracks of their rifles.

A searchlight from the camp immediately swept the area, but it was too far away for the rebels to knock out.

The mujahideen bullets appeared to have little more than a mosquito effect on the enemy position. Intermittently, the Russians would fire off a brief burst from a heavy machine gun or would send up a flare. But it was only token.

Disregarding our group, several tanks began rumbling toward the northern part of the town where [other] mujahideen were proving to be a nuisance.

Filtering back, the mujahideen did not seem to be perturbed by their obvious lack of strike capability. Throwing all caution to the wind and chatting like schoolboys after a football match, they discussed their "attack." No one had been injured and it was doubtful that they had inflicted any damage on the Russians.[15]

Mujahid attacks, large and small, have frequently been more effective than the two described here. While Girardet's group was making little impression at Jalalabad, others were attacking at the same time and got a stronger Soviet response. But throughout most of the country really ambitious maneuvers still remain beyond the guerrillas' capabilities. The reportedly large massing of mujahidin around Kabul in early June 1980 appears to have been intended more as a show of strength, and perhaps as a device to infiltrate the capital, than as a prelude to an attack on the four Soviet divisions there, which were no doubt eager for a frontal assault.

The resistance's ability to hold territory against small modern units has so far been limited to the Badakhshan/Takhar area and possibly the Pich Valley, between Kunar and Laghman provinces, where seesaw fighting came to a standstill in May and June. But despite the weakness and ineffectiveness of many of the groups engaged in hit-and-run raids, the command structure of the resistance has developed greatly since the Soviet invasion. Before its command was tested by a major Soviet thrust in late July, the Hizb-i-Islami organization south of Kandahar controlled a force of 12,000.[16] Barry Came of *Newsweek* reported a Hizb-i-Islami command of similar size actively fighting in the Kama district of Nangarhar province.[17] Even allowing for considerable exaggeration, these reports indicate great organizational advance over the few thousand fighters controlled by the

Hizb-i-Islami headquarters a few months before the invasion. The Hizb-i-Islami's command structure now extends across the country to include Herat and semiclandestine bases inside Iran's eastern border. Similar growth in size and capability has been accomplished by its fundamentalist rival, the Jamiyat-i-Islami. Also active in the cities, the Jamiyat-i-Islami dominates resistance groups in Kunar and is influential in Badakhshan. Gailani's Pushtun front has also grown in size and effectiveness, but has remained confined to the eastern region south of Jalalabad. None of the other Peshawar-based organizations can claim more than 1,000 active mujahidin.

The three main groups, with their increased capacity to wage war, are in a position to make major changes in the political as well as the tactical impact of the resistance. The Soviet menace is itself the primary cause of this growing cohesion. The largest resistance organizations now have the command structure and the manpower to begin to attempt more ambitious and precisely mounted attacks. Their component units are now strong enough to overawe or overrun small detachments of Soviet or Afghan government troops, which have had to be increasingly withdrawn from the countryside in favor of occasional sweeps by larger mobile units.

Despite such development of its capacity to inflict damage, the resistance continues to suffer from a lack of effective coordination of its major organizations. The Soviet forces have yet to face combined operations in the field which would permit the resistance to strike simultaneously at several points or to isolate exposed units by tying down Soviet mobile or reserve forces elsewhere.

As the resistance has grown stronger and the Soviet presence more galling, Afghan army units have become increasingly inclined to join the mujahidin. Negotiations between mujahidin and commanders of the more remote garrisons have become commonplace. Agreements on sudden joint operations against nearby Soviet troops and provincial capitals have produced some of the greatest resistance successes: the seizure of Bamiyan, part of the Panjshir Valley, and the Faizabad airport.

145

The village of Abdar, in the Panjshir Valley

The Soviet defense of Jalalabad has been complicated by the subversion of Afghan units. By early spring, after mutinies and desertions, the Ninth Division virtually disappeared.

Terror has inevitably become a tactic of the resistance. Assassination of government officials, Marxists, schoolteachers, and their families has become standard practice. Their homes are identified and systematically destroyed. As a result, the Parcham government has been effectively denied contact (except by force) with the population nearly everywhere. Without elaborate precautions, travel by officials has become hazardous even within Kabul.

Resistance terror also extends to the Russians, all of whom, civilians as well as soldiers, are considered to be legitimate targets. The mujahid groups take no prisoners. Apart from the logistical problems that prisoners would present, they are seen as infidel intruders, unworthy of mercy. Summary execution of Russians has had an inhibiting effect on Soviet tactics. Their attacks tend to be tightly massed under heavy mechanized protection. To some extent their operations have been hindered by their unwillingness to send out small patrols that would make easy targets.

The refusal to take prisoners has hurt the resistance cause in the court of world opinion. Coupled with reports of barbaric acts, such as the torture and mutilation of the Russians caught at Herat in March 1979, the killing of all captured Russian soldiers conveys an impression of rabid fanaticism, which tends to dilute sympathy for the cause of Afghan national resistance. Such brutal acts must be measured against the suffering being caused by the Soviet forces through their immense superiority in weapons of destruction and their lack of restraint in unleashing them on a largely defenseless population.

The willingness of the Kabul government and its Soviet backers to use terror was most tragically demonstrated by the massacre of more than 1,100 men and boys of Kyrala (Kerala), a large village in the Kunar Valley, in April 1979. Rounded up and surrounded by Afghan soldiers and their Russian advisers, the victims were told to shout out their support of the Khalq government. When they refused, they were machine-gunned and buried, dead and dying, in a mass grave by bulldozers. The methodical manner in which this slaughter was carried out clearly indicates that it had been planned. The women and children, who had been herded into the village mosque, and the few surviving men escaped to Pakistan, where they reported the massacre to numerous journalists.

Since the Soviet invasion, at least one village has been massacred. In retaliation for an attack on a small group of soldiers, a village near Kunduz was leveled and its 600 people were killed in May 1980.[18]

Realistic casualty figures cannot be expected to come from a country that has never taken a complete census. In early March 1980 one resistance spokesman put the number of Afghan dead in fighting since the April 1978 coup at 110,000.[19] This figure

147

The Kunduz Valley

would seem to be much closer to the actual number than the claims of more than one million dead made by other resistance spokesmen. The rising intensity and scope of hostilities and punitive raids almost certainly have accelerated the casualty rate since Soviet forces became directly involved.

Death directly caused by physical attacks accounts for a small part of the human cost. Given the virtual absence of medical facilities for the resistance and the general population, death and grave disability from injuries that cannot be treated are pervasive. Illness, exhaustion, and exposure during flight may well have caused more casualties than actual attacks.

Fighting, bombing, and persecution forced nearly 400,000 Afghans to seek refuge in Pakistan before the Soviet invasion. Within the next five months the refugee population there doubled. At least 100,000, perhaps 300,000, found sanctuary in

Iran, even though it did not operate an official relief program. The suffering that these numbers imply was greatly aggravated by severe winter conditions. Olaf Ihlau, writing in the *Suddeutsche Zeitung*, describes the condition of Pushtun refugees who reached Pakistan within the first weeks of the invasion:

"For Allah's sake, please help us. We are freezing and starving," coughs a Pathan [Pushtun] warrior perhaps fifty-five years old, his face streaked with tears, gnarled hands holding a mustard-colored turban thrust through the jeep window as a ragged begging bowl. He is shaking with cold early in the morning at the Pakistani registration center at Parachinar, in the border province of Kurram. . . . Pakistan is unable to cope with the refugees. A model tent city of 7,000 near Peshawar is shown to visiting dignitaries, but most refugees have no tents, blankets, flour, or medical supplies. A few huts just below the snowline, fashioned out of straw mats, reeds, branches, and sheets, cannot protect them from the icy cold. People press together for warmth, but many of the weakest—mostly children—do not survive.

In one of the huts, at the feet of a pretty Pathan woman of about thirty, lies a squalling three-month-old girl swaddled in a basket. In her arms the mother holds a three-year-old son suffering from fever and severe diarrhea. Since fleeing their village, the woman, Fatima, and her husband, Muhammad, have lost three of their six young children to exhaustion, pneumonia, and exposure.[20]

Soviet objectives have been extended from saving the Kabul government to destroying the resistance by terrorizing the population. A corollary goal appears to be the depopulation of regions where resistance has been especially stubborn, primarily by forcing the people to flee.

Against the Soviets' modern weapons and tactics, the freedom fighters have used their difficult countryside, their expertise with light weapons, the cover of night, the support of the population, their own incredible hardiness and stamina, their talent for improvisation, and a growing ability to organize. Animating and motivating their actions has been a mixture of dedication and fatalism unique to Islam. It engenders a willingness to die or to accept the anguish of cold, hunger, untreated

Men praying at the entrance to a mosque in Istalif, near Kabul

wounds, and the loss of loved ones in defense of their way of life, which is identified with their religion. Islam as the governing inspiration has been extended to include Afghan nationhood. Hence the acceptance of the mission of the holy warrior against the infidel who would destroy what is virtuous and meaningful. To die in such a cause is an act of grace; to suffer, an act of virtue. Thus motivated, the whole population has faced massacre, devastating weapons it has no means of coping with, and the presence of a superpower with seemingly limitless sources of manpower and firepower without slackening its resistance. This defiance has vindicated the claim of Gailani: "If the Russians invade, they will die here. No matter how big an army they send, we will not lay down our arms until Afghanistan belongs to her people again."[21]

This conviction was echoed by Mengal Hussein, speaking for the Hizb-i-Islami: "You must understand that we are fighting a holy war according to our Islamic duties. Several Soviet divisions do not worry us."[22]

The willingness to sacrifice oneself in the resistance cause—children running up to Soviet tanks to obscure the view of the Russians inside by throwing mud on their windows, mothers with children in their arms inviting soldiers to shoot, old men and women volunteering to throw themselves under tanks with satchel charges—such self-sacrificing behavior expresses the courage and determination that have made the Afghans' primitive tactics far more effective than the Russians and outside observers had expected.

Such an implacable resistance has cast serious doubt on the ability of the Soviet forces to achieve pacification without resorting to techniques approaching genocide. It has been estimated that in order to exert enough pressure against all regions of resistance, the Soviets would have at least to triple the manpower they committed to the initial invasion.[23] Despite its vast army, the Soviet Union would feel considerable strain—economic, strategic, and moral—if it attempted to maintain such a level of force indefinitely. Such an effort would materially cut into the resources available to continue the comprehensive building of

Soviet military capabilities, which was given high priority in the 1970s. Protracted antiguerrilla war threatens to overextend the Soviets' military resources as long as they remain committed to involvement in Vietnam, Cambodia, Cuba, Ethiopia, Angola, and South Yemen; to building a navy to rival that of the United States; to maintaining nuclear and strategic parity; to retaining control over restive Eastern Europe; and to securing their long and sensitive border with China. These vast commitments, coupled with the sluggish rigidity of the Soviet economy, prevent the USSR from undertaking such an unlimited investment.

Escalation of its effort would require the Soviet Union to pour in men and matériel out of all proportion to Afghanistan's significance as a security factor. In so concentrating forces along less than 15 percent of its boundaries, the Soviet command dilutes its strength elsewhere and tends to throw its defensive posture out of balance. This imbalance can be expected to be brought home to the Soviet people by growing battle casualties. Casualties were not officially admitted until nearly five months after the invasion. No comprehensive figures have been published, and strenuous attempts have been made to isolate the wounded by restricting them to military hospitals as far from European Russia as possible. Most have been treated in Central Asian or East German hospitals.[24] These measures may have delayed popular response to the human costs of the invasion, but the attempts to mask and downplay them are likely to backfire. The Soviet public has much experience with official manipulation of bad news. Attempts to hide casualties can lead to rumors that could magnify losses beyond the grim reality. In waging a long-term war, the Soviet government could find that an attempt to disguise its losses will critically undermine popular acceptance, especially in view of the patent fact that Afghanistan has never threatened the Soviet Union and indeed had enjoyed highly publicized friendly relations with it since 1955.

Estimates of the casualties suffered by the Soviet forces vary widely. At the end of May 1980, resistance spokesmen put the number of Russian dead at 7,000 to 10,000. Western analysts generally put the figure at one-tenth of that number.[25] A State

Department estimate in April put the weekly casualty rate at 800, with deaths averaging 15 percent.[26] The circumstances of casualty losses were shifting from isolated attacks by civilians and by rebellious Afghan army units to battles waged by mujahid groups. After February, as fighting intensified in Kunar, Paktia, Herat, and Bamiyan provinces, the rate of Russian casualties certainly increased. Such regional struggles still continue to determine the course of the war.

Regional Patterns of Resistance

Resistance against the Russians and their Parcham clients has risen virtually everywhere, among every major ethnic, sectarian, and regional group. Student groups, Afghan army units, city mobs, and individual citizens as well as guerrilla units have taken part in the fighting. Reports of these struggles have been extremely uneven. It has been much easier to uncover information on the fighting in the larger cities and in the Pushtun regions in the east and southeast than on the conflicts in the rest of the country. As a result an impression has been given unwittingly that the fiercest fighting has involved Pushtuns. Actions by the Soviet forces and the Parcham government have also attracted a disproportionate share of journalists' attention. The overall impression that the resistance and hostilities have been concentrated in limited areas is misleading. The fragmentary evidence available suggests that the Communist forces have less control in the Hazarajat than elsewhere and that their authority has been sharply contested from Farah to Mazar-i-Sharif to Badakhshan as well as in the Pushtun-dominated regions. By mid-1980, distinctive patterns of opposition had developed in the various parts of the country and in the major cities.

The Northeast: Badakhshan, Takhar, Kunduz, and Baghlan Provinces

Resistance forces have had their greatest successes in seizing and holding contested territory and besieging small towns in the northeast. Tajik and Uzbek insurgents continued to surround

153

the provincial capitals of Faizabad, Taloqan, Kunduz, and Baghlan after the invasion, despite the proximity of the Soviet border. Foreign journalists have rarely been able to reach this remote and difficult area. Reports have depended almost entirely on resistance networks, especially those of the Jamiyat-i-Islami and the Hizb-i-Islami.

The Pamirs, a region of high-altitude valleys surrounded by lofty peaks, bar the population of these provinces from safety in Pakistan. Fired by hatred of the Soviets, who had driven much of the local population into Afghanistan as refugees in the 1920s, the Uzbeks and Tajiks had little choice or desire but to stand and fight. Even when allowance is made for exaggeration, their effectiveness is evident. Sharp attacks were launched in January against the Russian-supported Afghan army garrisons at Faizabad, Taloqan, and several smaller towns. In response, Soviet units were rushed in from bases just across the border. Battles for these remote places were waged savagely throughout the winter. Aided by defecting army units, the insurgents briefly held Taloqan and the Faizabad air base. The Soviets found it almost impossible to open land routes into the area. Tanks and armored personnel carriers could easily be mined, ambushed, or blocked by landslides along the tortuous mountain roads.

The insurgents have consolidated their control over the rugged terrain of Badakhshan and Takhar and have spread their attacks into adjacent Kunduz and Baghlan provinces. In mid-March the city of Baghlan was assaulted and at the end of the month a force of several thousand mujahidin swept through the industrial center of Kunduz. These attacks threatened to cut off the main north–south highway between the Soviet Union and Kabul. Counterattacks drove the insurgents out of these cities, but throughout the spring they continued to control much of the lowlands as well as all of the mountain areas of the region. Heavy bombing of villages has been the most effective of the Soviet responses. Reports of the use of gas by the Russians in the steep and narrow valleys of Badakhshan and Takhar, where most of the intense fighting has been concentrated, have also been numerous.

The East: Laghman, Kunar, and Nangarhar Provinces

Soviet troops also became quickly involved in the strategic eastern zone. Jalalabad, in Nangarhar province, is located at the center of the area. It is on the main Kabul–Khyber Pass highway, forty miles from the Pakistani border. Just outside the city the Kunar River, flowing from the northeast, joins the Kabul River. Fighting has been focused in the Kunar Valley and Jalalabad. Within a week of the invasion Soviet troops took over the defense of the city. Its airfield quickly became jammed with helicopters, MiGs, and transport planes; the highway from Kabul could not be depended on for the transport of supplies because the resistance repeatedly cut off traffic.

Jalalabad is situated in a lowland plain broken by scattered hills, with high mountains behind them on all sides providing cover and sanctuary for quick attacks by small groups. Pushtun communities in this area traditionally supplemented their income by exacting tribute from the traffic moving to and from the city.

Pacification of the area is greatly complicated by its ready access to Pakistan. By slipping over the border, mujahidin can evade assaults launched from the city. Their contacts there also permit them to resupply and reorganize themselves. Sealing off the border or at least making passage difficult thus became a main objective of the Soviets. They saw the Kunar Valley as the most active corridor of resistance supply. Earlier, Amin's troops had unsuccessfully tried to garrison the valley, but they had been either run off or bottled up in the small towns along the river.

These Afghan units now became a further source of trouble for the Soviets. Just before Soviet troops arrived, the Afghan garrison besieged at Barikot, on the Pakistani border in upper Kunar, mutinied and went over to the resistance. More alarming was the desertion of most of the Jalalabad garrison, which fought the Russians at the beginning of January and then dissolved into the hills. In early February there was further defection among troops supporting the two Soviet divisions in the

East meets West in Jalalabad

area. Friction grew as a result of Soviet contempt for the Afghan troops and fear of their treachery.

During January and February the Soviets built up air and armored strength at Jalalabad and probed the resistance with light ground sorties. On February 29 they launched their first offensive up the Kunar Valley. Joint air and armored sweeps sent the insurgents scurrying for the hills and caused heavy casualties in the villages along the river. A new surge of refugees trekked toward Pakistan. The Soviets easily won control over the valley floor, but the struggle was far from over, as David DeVoss described for *Time*:

> With few large bridges or population centers, Kunar does not lend itself to mechanized warfare. But the fact has not deterred the Soviet juggernaut. Few towns lying near the sinuous Kunar River have escaped. Chenar and Dangam, first bombed by MiGs, were later also hit by rocket-firing helicopters. The exodus of 6,000 refugees from Kunar into Pakistan has left the area between the border and the river eerily quiet. But the hills have not been abandoned. No mountain is without its militia. After escorting their women into Pakistan, most men return, climb a few thousand feet higher and join one of the scattered rebel packs.[27]

The announced purpose of the offensive was to seal off Kunar province from the supplies and refuge to be found in Pakistan. For several weeks the mujahidin were on the defensive. Suffering from the late-winter cold in the hills, short of food, and lacking weapons effective against helicopters, armor, and artillery, the mujahidin were limited to harassing night attacks against Soviet troops who were now dug in. Yet the drive did not achieve its goal of cutting off the guerrillas' access to Pakistan; they simply shifted to other routes. Their attacks on Jalalabad continued. On several occasions they were able to cut off its power supply and block highway traffic.

In April the Soviets spread their annihilation campaigns into the valleys of Laghman and Nangarhar provinces. Their shock tactics again brought heavy civilian casualties but did not reduce resistance activity. Thinned out over the three-province area, the two Soviet divisions became exposed to counterattacks. Seesaw battles went on for Chigha Sarai, on the Kunar River; for the Pich Valley, which connects Kunar with Laghman; and for the Kama Valley, between Jalalabad and the Khyber Pass. Four months after these heavy attacks, the Soviets' hold on the region remained insecure and contested. By late May, mujahid assaults on outposts in Kunar were increasingly successful, as this description in *Asiaweek* indicates:

> The fighting on the heights at Taipar Ghundai had started about 9 A.M. and the communist forces at the mountaintop base in Afghanistan's Kunar Province were getting the worst of it. The fortification in the bunkered compound, manned by about 160 Afghans and five Soviet advisers in Afghan Army uniform, had been completed only 20 days earlier. Some 200 mujahiddin, Islamic guerrillas, armed with captured Soviet weapons and supported by a 4,000 man second line carrying locally made 303 Lee Enfield copies, had now come within grenade distance on three sides and silenced the defenders' heavy machine guns.
>
> Suddenly, shortly after noon, some government soldiers began running away. Others waved their weapons in surrender, then threw them aside. Over the compound's low stone wall the guerrillas leapt, shouting "Allah-o-akhbar! Allah-o-akhbar!" (God is great!).[28]

Soviet and Parcham troubles in Kunar extend beyond such small defeats. As *Asiaweek* reported:

> During the so-called "early spring offensive" in this area, the Afghan 30th Mountain Brigade went over to the mujahiddin, raising the quality of rebel activity in the province. In March, the Russians and Afghans suffered embarrassing setbacks when they tried to open the Pich Valley linking Kunar with Laghman. After three days of heavy fighting, the mujahiddin captured an Afghan battalion, and the communist forces were obliged to retreat to the provincial capital. . . .[29]

Reports on the struggle for this region since the invasion have been silent on the role of the Nuristanis, whose revolt against the

Taraki/Amin regime originally triggered the fighting there. It is highly unlikely that they have escaped involvement in the fighting in Kunar and Laghman or have been free from air attacks, which began before Soviet forces were on the scene. This silence is probably the result of the Nuristanis' integration into other resistance groups and the much greater publicity generated by the Pushtun-dominated groups headquartered in Pakistan.

The Southeast: Kandahar, Ghazni, Paktia, and Zabul Provinces

Hostilities developed more slowly in the southeast than they did in the north. Soviet troops reached Kandahar on January 1, but throughout the winter, action was limited to light skirmishes. The Soviet command placed a lower priority on the area, partly because resistance activity had been limited there, despite the region's reputation as the traditional stronghold of the great Ghilzai and Durrani tribes and of the smaller but fierce Mohmand, Mangal, and Waziri groups of Paktia. The area presents forbidding obstacles to military control. Its southern half is mostly a rocky, hilly desert wilderness; its eastern flank offers a rugged wooded area for guerrilla cover. The troops available to the Soviet command are too few for deployment over its large area.

Resistance groups have also been widely scattered. Neither side concentrated much force against the other until fighting flared up in April at Qarabagh, near the main highway south of Ghazni, and then at Ghazni itself in July as the result of violent clashes between an Afghan garrison and Soviet troops. The Hizb-i-Islami has almost monopolized the organization of the resistance in the region. Its efforts have been concentrated on cutting the main highway on either side of Kandahar. The western section leading to Herat has been frequently cut near Girishk.

Punishing air attacks have been directed at villages throughout Paktia and along the Kabul–Kandahar highway. Ground action has been limited, but given the region's large reservoir of insurgent manpower and the failure of the Russians to control the highways, it cannot be expected to remain so relatively inac-

A walled section of Ghazni

tive for long. Meanwhile its Hizb-i-Islami bands are untested. Anthony Paul's description of mujahid preparations hints at what may be ahead for them:

> I have been in Guerrilla Commander Zafarruddin's headquarters camp now for three days and I'm bothered by something: there's no attempt at camouflage. I've been living in one of about 20 conspicuous white tents scattered across the brown earth. . . . Standing amongst us are even more obvious signs of the military presence here: a couple of howitzers, 10 wheeled Russian-built Craz trucks, two armoured personnel carriers. At the airfield at Spin Baldak, a short jet hop away, . . . the Russians have 50 helicopters, 25 jets, 400 to 500 tanks.
>
> "What plans, then, do the mujahidin have for guarding against aerial reconnaissance and attack?" I ask the young officer. The question takes an unexpectedly long time for translation. . . . "The Commander is saying that when the Russian jets are coming, his forward defense line telephones him. Immediately, he puts bushes on the tops of his tents."[30]

The West: Farah, Herat, Nimroz, and Badghis Provinces

Resistance throughout the wide arc from the Sistan swamps in Nimroz to the rolling hills and grazing country of Badghis has gone almost without reporting. Guerrilla groups in the west have not been able to develop in Iran the same sort of international press connections that the eastern groups have developed in Pakistan. Afghans—a mixture of mujahidin, destitute refugees, nomads, and smugglers following traditional paths—have been moving back and forth across the mostly unpatrolled border in large numbers. The close community ties across the border enable all of them to move with little interference.

Soviet units stationed in the region are concentrated at Herat and at Shindand Air Force Base. Elements of an army division are also stationed between Herat and Farah and the Iranian border.

Insurgent activity in the vast open spaces of this region has gone on intermittently since January 1980, when small groups attempted to cut the Kandahar–Herat highway on both sides of

The Struggle for Afghanistan

Farah. Throughout the winter and spring of 1980 mujahidin were active in the hills near Shindand. The most noted resistance has continued to come from Herat city and its surrounding valley. Jonathan Kwitney's description of antigovernment feeling in a Herat village applies to most of the country and indicates a level of resistance in this region which has gone largely unnoticed:

> The government apparently has given up trying to control the villages, at least for the moment [January 1980]. Officials are careful not to stray from the main roads and they deny a reporter authority to do so, saying it is too dangerous. In fact it is only dangerous for the officials. This reporter, without permission, easily went into the small villages off the main road, escorted by antigovernment sympathizers. The reception was always warm.[31]

In June reports of a major Soviet pacification drive in the Herat sector filtered out. This drive failed to dislodge the mujahidin, who took large sections of the city in late July. Once again, Herat became a no-man's-land.

The North: Faryab, Jozjan, Balkh, and Samangan Provinces

Even less has been heard from the provinces west of Kunduz and north of the Hindu Kush. Soviet troop presence has been light, but units have been massed on the Soviet side of the border just to the north. Mujahidin are most active in the hills that rise in the southern halves of these provinces. Some have harassed Mazar-i-Sharif, the largest city in the region, in night raids. Resistance groups claimed that they broke the natural gas pipeline supplying the Soviet Union in early June. In August came reports of insurgent horsemen rampaging freely in the open plains of Jozjan and Faryab, of fighting for the highway town of Samangan, and of mujahidin routed near Khulm.[32]

The Central Highlands (the Hazarajat): Ghor, Bamiyan, and Uruzgan Provinces

There has been virtually no penetration by government or Soviet authority into the mountain wilderness of the Hazarajat.

No paved road enters it, and until May of each year motorized travel is nearly impossible. During the Khalq regime the Hazaras and smaller minorities of the region had essentially cut themselves off from Kabul. This state of affairs continues, disturbed by occasional bombing sorties and feeble attempts to maintain government control of the provincial capitals of Bamiyan and Chakhcharan. There has been no attempt to show the flag at Uruzgan.

Reports from this area are also rare and usually come secondhand from resistance sources. A Soviet convoy attempting to move south through Bamiyan was ambushed and routed in early January. Later a provincial governor was installed at Bamiyan, but he and his staff were reported killed when his Afghan garrison mutinied at the end of May and went over to the resistance.[33] The governor of Ghor suffered a similar fate in March.[34]

Except for Bamiyan, with its extraordinary archaeological and tourist interest and relative closeness to Kabul and the main road system, the region is likely to be ignored by the Communist authorities. Resistance groups have established a regional government based on local and tribal divisions and customs.

The Kabul Axis: Kabul, Parwan, Wardak, Kapisa, and Logar Provinces

The provinces surrounding Kabul are crucial to the immediate security of the government. Most of the country's modern economic, administrative, and educational institutions are clustered in this region. Its extensive valleys, stretching from Kohdaman and Kapisa in the north to Logar in the south, are the country's most fertile and productive. The Soviet presence in the area has been large and highly visible. The Begram air base in Parwan is the headquarters of the Soviet air units. Kabul itself is ringed by Soviet army units, which have dug themselves in along all of the major approach highways. Eric Abraham described conditions near the city in late March:

Nothing is more noticeable as you drive through the villages on the outskirts of Kabul than the absence of young men—who, some say,

Boy with melon, Bamiyan

Girl, Bamiyan

A *qala* (fortress home) in the Logar Valley

have taken to the hills to join the rebels. Also significant is the fact that the turrets of the Soviet tanks face the villages, ready for any outbreak of resistance. In the city, too—particularly in the old part near the bazaars—tanks and armoured personnel carriers are positioned at each cross-section, public building and bridge.[35]

Resistance activity in this region is extremely hazardous for the insurgents and threatening to the government and the Russians. In view of the difficulties of operating in such a closely defended area, resistance activity has been remarkably extensive, and it has expanded since the end of the winter of 1980.

Small attacks, usually at night, began in January, especially in Parwan and Logar. The main north–south highway was briefly blocked south of the Salang Pass and a Soviet supply convoy was ambushed.[36] There was skirmishing in Charikar, the capital of

Parwan. In February the Salang Pass tunnel was briefly blocked.[37] Small insurgent groups roamed near Kabul during the late winter. During the week-long general strike in Kabul at the end of February, resistance groups were active and had effective access to the city.

After the severe winter the pace of resistance quickened. An attack on the base at Begram in early April reportedly caused heavy Soviet casualties, among them a general.[38] Later in the month the new Soviet-assisted copper mine in the Logar Valley was blown up and the Khairkhana ammunition and fuel dump, just outside Kabul, was bombed.[39]

By early June regional resistance groups were ready to make a show of strength in the environs of Kabul. They assembled in a semicircle north, west, and south of the city to make a series of hit-and-run attacks from the cover of the nearby Paghman and Kohistan mountains in the face of four Soviet divisions, which were hastily reinforced by air. Probing the Paghman Valley and the Kargha sector, just west of Kabul, the guerrillas claimed successful attacks against small Afghan army detachments and the seizure of equipment. Several hundred mujahidin apparently slipped into the city through the Soviet defenses. Pounded by retaliatory air and armored attacks, especially in Kohdaman, northwest of Kabul, the main insurgent forces withdrew into the countryside.[40]

In late August the Soviets launched an attack up the Panjshir Valley. Reequipped and better organized, they fought their way up its canyon. On September 19 the Associated Press reported that

> the Soviets were sending reinforcements . . . and bombarding villages in possible preparation for an attempt to penetrate deeper. . . .
>
> Despite heavy casualties and losses of tanks, armored vehicles and helicopters, the Soviets secured daytime control of the winding dirt road to Rokha (24 miles up the valley) and cleared it of boulders that insurgents blasted down the mountainsides. . . .
>
> Afghans fleeing the valley said women were fighting alongside their husbands and brothers on the rebel side. . . .[41]

The Kohdaman Valley, from Istalif

Resistance in the Cities

Most urban Afghans found themselves almost literally living under the gun before the Soviet invasion. Since then their situation has become even more perilous. The major cities are surrounded by new Russian encampments whose field guns are usually trained on them. As its police force has become less reliable, the Parcham government has turned to a largely undisciplined and ill-trained armed "citizen" militia to enforce order in the cities. Its arbitrary power is an instrument of terror. Nighttime curfews are also designed to create terror. They are enforced by Soviet troops, who are kept from the cities during the daytime as a result of the series of ugly incidents soon after the invasion. Huge armored personnel carriers clamor through

168

Hunter, Panjshir Valley

the streets with more than enough firepower to render unrecognizable any errant civilian caught outside his home.

These instruments of terror are reinforced by the use of plain-clothes secret police, informers, and schoolchildren to control, confuse, and monitor neighborhoods and individuals. Kabulis, especially, are exposed to the small minority of Afghans who support the government. City youths are suddenly prominent in unprecedented ways. They have power as militiamen, demonstrators, enforcers, informers, and even as middle- and sometimes senior-level officials in posts suddenly vacated by the exigencies of the "revolution." In an atmosphere of such abrupt change, fear and anxiety vie with contempt, anger, and incomprehension.

The responses of Afghan city dwellers have run the gamut from frenzied outbursts against any sign of authority to cautious conformity. Within weeks of the invasion the resistance groups took advantage of the urban agonies to foment violent defiance. The city dwellers' capacity for uprisings appears far from exhausted. The invasion brought great changes to the cities. Only Herat rose against Khalq; all of them now struggle against Parcham and the Russians.

Kandahar began the urban outbursts against the invasion on December 31, 1979, even before the Russians arrived there. Shops were locked up in a show of defiance and mobs attacked every manifestation of government: police stations, public buildings, Afghan troops. Three Russian civilians who worked for the United Nations were attacked while shopping in the bazaar and murdered. Afghan army reinforcements were rushed in and the city was quiet when the first Soviet detachments arrived the next day.[42] They prudently bivouacked at the American-built airport and stayed out of town.

The Kandahar riot included elements that reappeared in outbursts in other cities: the closing of the bazaar as a signal for mass protests, attacks on government personnel, hostile actions against Russians (sometimes directed toward other Europeans by mistake), and a willingness to risk death or injury from heavily armed troops.

170

A teahouse in Kabul

What the Kandahar uprising lacked in December—clear objectives and organized action—was to be supplied at Herat within a month. In late January 1980 a general strike paralyzed the city. Again the people massed in the streets. Their demonstrations lasted a week. Organization was evident in the avoidance of violence and in the introduction of a uniquely Afghan instrument of protest, the rooftop chant. "Allah-o-akbar" (God is great) was cried out over the whole city just after dusk for several hours each night.[43] These forms of protest spread back to Kandahar at the beginning of February and flared up in Jalalabad and Baghlan by the middle of the month.[44]

Kabul, meanwhile, had been sullenly quiet if not peaceful. Detachments of rebellious Afghan troops had held out in the suburbs until mid-January, when they were destroyed by air attacks. In the meantime perhaps as many as a dozen Russian soldiers had been killed in encounters with civilians. During this period there also were reports of numerous assassinations of Parcham officials and their relatives.

Kabul's tension was unleashed on February 21, when the bazaar shut down. The resistance groups worked together to stage a crippling general strike. *Shabnamas* (night letters) calling for demonstrations against the government were distributed during the curfew hours. The following day, a Friday—the Muslim sabbath—brought mobs into the streets, especially those of the old city. They quickly overran police and militia strong points, raided police arsenals, and marched on local Afghan army posts, calling on the soldiers to join them. Some from the Kargha barracks did. Parchamists were hunted down. In the early stages of the street fighting the police and some military units became demoralized by the fury of the demonstrators.[45] Men are reported to have walked up to Afghan soldiers, one after the other, asking to be shot. After shooting several, the soldiers ran away, unnerved.[46]

Government control over most of the city was quickly lost. Soviet armored units were brought in. Some of their tanks and APCs were overwhelmed by mobs in narrow lanes, but they succeeded in clearing the streets by machine-gunning and ramming the crowds. The numbers of reported deaths on February 22 run as high as 500.

The Russian commander of the Kabul area declared martial law. The Soviet embassy complex, in the southeast suburbs, was cordoned off. Karmal and his colleagues took refuge there and were not seen during the uprising, even on television. Shops remained closed and a government strike continued until February 29. Kabul's citizens also took to their roofs and called out for divine help. An informed resident of the city describes the scene: "Thursday night, February 21, was unforgettable: it was the night of the shut-down of all the shops in the city. About

10 that evening we heard something outside, went out, and from all parts of the city, near and far, we could hear 'Allah-o-akbar' from thousands of citizens. It was a wet, misty night, with halos around the street lights, and only this powerful sound ringing through the silent city. It was spine-tingling. We all knew, then, that Kabul would rise when the time came."[47]

As the strike lost momentum, young Parcham militiamen reappeared and began to make arrests. The Hazara neighborhood in the old city was given special attention. A Shia minority, the Hazaras served as convenient scapegoats. Many other Kabulis, including a large number of children who had defied the tanks, were arrested. The militiamen had powers of summary trial and execution. Rumors had the total killed as high as 1,500. Diplomatic sources put those arrested at 2,000; most were released within a few days. Kabul Radio and the Soviet press declared that foreign provocateurs were responsible for the trouble. Twenty-one foreigners were arrested: sixteen Pakistanis, two Chinese, two Americans, and one Egyptian. One of the Americans, David Lee, confessed his complicity on Afghan television. A released Australian prisoner claims he witnessed the psychological and physical pressure at Puli Charkhi prison which induced Lee to talk.[48]

Under the militia's reign of terror the city quieted. New shabnamas called for demonstrations on the Islamic New Year, March 21, but the day passed without serious incident.

During the turmoil in Kabul, strikes and demonstrations were reported in Jalalabad, Wardak, Kandahar, Baghlan, and Herat. Strikes recurred in Herat in mid-March. A month later student agitation flared through the streets of Kunduz. Resistance flared through nearly all of the cities, shaking Parcham's already feeble grasp.

Public demonstrations were held again in Kabul, this time by the students, whose role in the February uprising had been small.[49] The occasion was the Parcham government's attempt to celebrate the second anniversary of the April 27 coup. VIPs from the Soviet bloc were flown in, Kabul was cleaned up, and a program of public rallies and parades was scheduled. The opportunity was taken to introduce a new national flag, which restored Islamic green and the old mosque emblem. Disputes between surviving Khalq hard-liners in the cabinet and the Parcham leadership, which wanted to accommodate Islam, spread to student factions at the university and in the high schools. Their arguments degenerated into violence. There was a new round of demonstrations, riots, and assassinations. Pro-Amin high school girls marched on the homes of the non-Marxist members of the cabinet and demanded their removal. Some of the demonstrators were shot by army sentries. Anti-Marxist female students demonstrated at the Ministry of the Interior and the presidential palace. They jeered the Afghan garrison, demanding that they shoot or join the resistance. The troops held their fire, but nearby Russians did not. In the high schools rival factions were killing each other. Factionalism and antigovernment demonstrations resulted in a strike that closed Kabul University in mid-April.

These disturbances culminated in five days of rioting on and off the campuses, from April 24 to 28. They were a great embarrassment to the government, which could not hide them from its foreign guests. Rocks and epithets were flung at passing limousines. At Habibiya, the largest boys' high school, which is on the same avenue as the Soviet embassy, thirteen students were killed by Russian security troops who were protecting the car of a Soviet Communist Party secretary, Mikhail Zimyanin. Greater casualties occurred when a helicopter gunship strafed demonstrators at the university campus. Altogether, some two hundred students were killed in the disturbances.

Yet student defiance reappeared only two weeks later. High school girls again escaped from their campuses—they are walled and had been placed under guard—to demonstrate against the minister of education, Dr. Anahita Ratebzad, the only woman in the Marxist cabinet. They demanded the release of 2,000 students who they claimed were still in prison after the earlier disturbances. This later spate of agitation was more peaceful, but after two weeks of constant protests more than a thousand new arrests had been made, mostly of girls. In early June mass

Students of Rabia Balkhi Lycée, Kabul

poisonings were reported at three girls' high schools; some students died.[50]

Student disturbances are particularly threatening to the Marxist authorities. A major share of their narrow support comes from students and recent graduates. They are a major source of reliable recruits for lower government positions and for the militia, the police, and the depleted military officer corps. Indoctrination through education is the government's main hope for eventually building a permanent base for its revolution. Convulsions between student Marxist factions also are a great danger to Parcham's fragile internal consensus. The spectacle of pro-Amin and pro-Karmal students killing each other gravely aggravated the internal rivalries within the government itself.

Student unrest is an explosive issue for urban Afghans generally. The students, practically by definition, form a significant and growing segment of the educated elite. Whatever prominent Kabulis think of the government, they are anxiously aware that the future of their families will be largely determined by the roles their student sons and daughters play in the situation created by the coup and the invasion. Caught between traditional loyalties and explosive modern change, young people are forced to decide which faction to support, whether to join the resistance, whether or how to avoid the life-and-death rivalries unleashed by repression and resistance. The very active role of schoolgirls in these anarchic conflicts demonstrates the latent capacity of Afghan women to become aggressively involved and even to dominate public events.

Future opportunities even for the wealthiest and best connected will depend on the directions and results of government-controlled education. The pivotal role of educated youth is already significant. An Afghan interviewed in the spring of 1980 explained that "students are effectively used for surveillance, for organizing the citizenry and for distributing propaganda."[51] Hence students, especially in Kabul, have great political leverage, which can be used for or against the government. The schoolgirl riots of April and May weakened an already shaky government. They made Russian control even more nakedly evident and left even fewer Afghans—particularly among the young—willing to support or accept Soviet interference.

The Role of the Afghan Armed Forces

Already demoralized and divided at the time of the Soviet invasion, the Afghan army (the air force no longer functions separately from Soviet units) has not been able to carry out the pacification tasks assigned to it. In late 1979 rivalries between pro- and anti-Amin units were already tearing the army apart. Within six months of the invasion the army had disintegrated further through continuous mutinies and defections, culminating in an open break between Khalq- and Parcham-oriented units in July 1980.

The Soviet pacification scheme assumed that the army could

Father and son, Kabul Gorge

be quickly revived after Karmal had been installed and Soviet troops had secured the cities. Afghan troops would then be free to suppress the resistance in the countryside. Indoctrination, partly through the training of a new group of young officers in the Soviet Union, was expected to produce a military force dedicated to the "revolution" and the crushing of guerrilla resistance. Soviet troops could then be withdrawn or kept at bases in reserve and out of contact with the Afghan people.

These expectations have been rudely dashed. Not only the disintegration of the Afghan army but the outright hostility of those units that have retained their capacity to fight have seriously upset the Soviets' calculations. As a result, their own troops have had to take up the uninviting task of rural pacification. Moreover, the Soviet authorities have found that hostile Afghan units are capable of inflicting heavy casualties on Russian troops and of seriously complicating efforts to maintain control in several regions of the country.

Much of this unforeseen difficulty stems from actions taken to divert or disarm Afghan units during the invasion itself. Units protecting Kabul and the main air bases were disarmed and confined to their barracks, usually through ruses that caught them unaware. One of the more clever was the removal of the batteries from the tanks of an Afghan armored unit on the pretext that they were faulty and that Soviet advisers had replacements. At Begram the banquet hoax was used: Afghan officers were locked in a room after Russian advisers had wined and dined them.

Despite such measures, units loyal to Amin fought arriving Soviet troops for control of Radio Afghanistan on December 27, and some reportedly fought for control of the streets of Kabul for three or four days, inflicting heavy casualties. Both the Parcham government and the Russians attempted to suppress reports of this fighting; journalists were not permitted entry into the country until the end of the first week of January.[52]

In Jalalabad the first of a series of clashes between Afghan and Soviet troops occurred as soon as the latter arrived. Afghan units sent there as reinforcements later mutinied. The most se-

Darulaman Palace, near Kabul

rious defections occurred in March and April, when troops
going over to resistance groups nearby took their equipment
with them.

Afghan troops were restive throughout the country. Soldiers
in Kandahar balked at suppressing the February strike in the
bazaar. As we saw earlier, some troops stationed at Kargha
joined the Kabul demonstrators. Also in February, an artillery
unit reportedly shelled the Begram air base and a regiment
mutinied in Herat. During the early stages of the offensive in
Kunar two Afghan brigades defected and were disarmed. An
artillery and an infantry brigade went over to the resistance in
Badakhshan and seized the Faizabad airport, though they could
not hold it.

Spring brought no improvement in the situation. In early
April a barracks uprising in Kabul cost the commander of the

Afghan army his job. In late May the garrison at Bamiyan killed local civilian officials and its own Soviet advisers and linked up with the local resistance.

Hostilities between Afghan and Soviet units reached a climax in mid-July, after Karmal moved to replace officers still loyal to Khalq. The result was a revolt by elements of the 10,000-man Fourteenth Armored Division stationed at Ghazni and an attempted coup by units at Puli Charkhi, just outside Kabul. The armored division had its full complement of equipment, artillery, anti-aircraft guns, and surface-to-air missiles. Soviet units surrounded and reportedly crushed the mutiny at Puli Charkhi, but two weeks of ground and air attacks against the Fourteenth Division had not destroyed the mutineers. The revolt reportedly spread from Ghazni to other Afghan units and involved contacts with the local resistance.[53]

The soldiers who have mutinied and defected have not always joined the resistance. But resistance units have frequently received the important benefits of supplies, the recruitment of trained officers and noncoms, and the distraction of the Russians, who have to treat "loyal" Afghan units with great caution. On numerous occasions individual Afghan soldiers have sprayed nearby Russians with bursts from automatic weapons. Even attempts to bring the two nationalities together can be dangerous, as when a joint celebration of the April Revolution in Kabul degenerated into a shootout after Afghan soldiers became enraged at the sight of pictures of Brezhnev on posters used as decorations.

The outbreaks of fighting in July indicate that so much friction exists between Russian and Afghan troops that the remaining Afghan units are more a liability than an asset in the struggle for Marxist control over Afghanistan. From this perspective, the fewer Afghan soldiers, the better. From an estimated 90,000 at the time of the invasion, the number of Afghan troops had dropped to 30,000 or fewer by June 1980. Yet if the disappearance of the Afghan army makes matters simpler for the Soviets, it aggravates their political situation seriously. It has forced the Soviet forces to function almost alone in repressing the popula-

Bamiyan countryside, from Shar-i-Gholghola

tion. With the Afghan army all but disintegrated, the Parcham government's claims that the Soviets are only a helpful ally becomes increasingly ludicrous. Accordingly, despite the dangers of issuing weapons to Afghans, the Kabul government began vigorous conscription in March.

It is possible that with careful recruitment and Soviet-assisted training of urban youths, an armed force reliably loyal to the government might eventually be created. Under the present circumstances of conflict within the Kabul government and hostility between Soviet and Afghan units, progress toward a more dependable national army seems doubtful. Failure to solve this problem would leave the Soviets in an increasingly vulnerable position, militarily and diplomatically.

The Prospects for the Resistance

For the freedom fighters to exert increasing pressure on the Kabul government and the Russians, they must develop an effective logistical and command structure capable of carrying out integrated operations throughout the countryside. Such a capability requires not only expertise in military organization and tactics suitable to their situation, but a considerable degree of political consensus and foreign support. Progress in these areas has so far been fitful and uncertain.

At the time of the invasion, links between the most active resistance groups fighting inside the country were tenuous and often shaped by traditional relationships among communities. Journalists trying to piece together the whole resistance picture reported between 60 and 200 groups separately involved in the fighting. Their connections with the Pakistan-based organizations that claim to speak for the resistance as a whole also were uncertain, especially those of mujahidin based outside of the Pushtun regions. This situation has changed considerably since the invasion. More and more resistance groups have aligned themselves with one or another of the Peshawar parties. To an increasing extent the more effective and aggressive of these parties have been able to recruit, supply, and command mujahidin inside Afghanistan.

The Soviet forces have provided a powerful stimulus for this tightening of organization. Survival against their aggressive search-and-destroy assaults has increasingly required intelligence and coordination. Consequently, the émigré groups best prepared to build links with the guerrillas have rapidly become the most prominent. Within the first several months of the struggle against the Russians, three have clearly stood out: the Hizb-i-Islami, with the largest following inside the country; the Jamiyat-i-Islami, which is powerful among the insurgents carrying the brunt of the fighting in Kunar; and Gailani's tribal coalition, prominent in Nangarhar and Paktia. Lacking a military command structure of its own, Mujadidi's Islamic National Front has lost ground in its efforts to unify the resistance. As the most aggressive émigré parties have built their organizations inside Afghanistan, they have been unwilling to let go of their own separately run external functions.

An immediate incentive for unification of the resistance has been the possibility of help from neighboring Muslim countries, especially through the Islamic Conference. It has met twice to discuss joint responses to the invasion, at a special emergency meeting in late January 1980 and at a foreign ministers' conference in May, both at Pakistan's capital, Islamabad. Representatives of these Muslim countries have made it clear that unification of the resistance is a prerequisite for significant material or political assistance.

Taking the lead in attempting to present a common front to the Islamic Conference was Burhanuddin Rabani, leader of the Jamiyat-i-Islami, who convened a meeting with the other Peshawar-based organizations to establish a single joint military command and to draft a common charter of objectives and commitments. The Islamic Conference gave them until early March to achieve their goals. No charter was forthcoming; with the exception of Mujadidi's Islamic National Front, each of the resistance organizations concentrated on building its own military apparatus. Gailani and Hekmatyar were especially successful in attracting their own funds from Persian Gulf sources.

Even so, negotiations went on between them continuously, and at the operational level cooperation grew. It was particularly notable in connection with the city uprisings. After the Hizb-i-Islami broke away from Rabani's alliance, Mujadidi retook the initiative and won agreement on a new Liberation Front to be led by Abdul Sayef, a young veteran of the Ikwan-i-Musalamin. Mujadidi accepted the vice-chairmanship of the organization. Gailani, Rabani, and leaders of the smaller organizations agreed to participate; Hekmatyar remained aloof.

Sayef led the Afghans who were seated at the May Islamic Conference as part of Iran's delegation. This arrangement permitted the Afghans to speak directly to the conference.

Meanwhile, an entirely new mechanism of participation and coordination was established for the resistance. In mid-May 916 representatives of groups fighting in all parts of Afghanistan met at Peshawar in a *momaselu loya jirgah*—provisional national council—which purported to represent all of the Afghan people. The jirgah had been called in early January with the support of the major Peshawar organizations. Loya jirgahs had been convened several times in the twentieth century as devices to win support for changes introduced by the Kabul government. Amanullah, Nadir Shah, Zahir Shah, and Muhammad Daoud had each called one. None had ever been called to organize a movement against an installed government, and consequently none had been held outside of the country.

Great pains were taken to make the jirgah representative. Each administrative district was to send three participants to ensure that at least one would get through to Peshawar. Of those that attended, thirty-five had sat in the national assembly that met in 1973. Muhammad Babrakzai, a former senior judge, was elected its chairman.

The jirgah proceeded to draft a forty-article provisional constitution for an Islamic republic that would be nonaligned and democratic. It set up a 110-member revolutionary council and several functional committees to establish operations in anticipation of a cabinet within a government in exile. The six largest resistance organizations were invited to name forty-two members of the council.[54]

Though the jirgah appears to have been a genuine attempt to blend traditional Afghan methods of government with a national organization capable of waging the struggle for liberation, most of the Peshawar leaders rejected it, claiming that it was unrepresentative of the Afghan people and illegitimate because it had been convened outside of the country. Only Gailani and Mujadidi favored it. Rivalries, vested interests, and differing visions of Afghanistan's future blocked coordinated action, at least temporarily. The immediate failure of the jirgah movement was a serious setback to Afghan unity. At the same time, the progress made by the Hizb-i-Islami and the Jamiyat-i-Islami account for much of the reason for opposition to it. Several months earlier the jirgah might have filled a vacuum. By May

1980 the largest organization had so greatly broadened and deepened their support that they had become serious contenders for eventual control of Afghanistan, after the hoped-for rout of the Russians. A jirgah-led resistance offered the chance for a consensus formula for eventual Afghan self-rule. It is not at all certain that its rejection is final, but the alternative to it would appear to be a struggle for power among the resistance groups which could delay or even destroy the chance for national liberation.

Given Soviet power and evident determination to master Afghanistan, such considerations may be brushed aside as theoretical. It is likely that a long struggle must be waged before any opportunity for liberation presents itself. In the course of that long process the resistance forces will have many opportunities to decide on some consensus formula, with or without a jirgah format. Resolution of their rivalries will depend on the appeal of their doctrines, the attractiveness of their leaders, their effectiveness on the battlefield, their links to the various ethnolinguistic communities, their ruthlessness, and their willingness to compromise. It will also depend on the outside support available to them. Should one or two organizations get the lion's share, they might overwhelm or absorb the rest.

Foreign support is vital to the chances for national liberation in any form. Without portable weapons effective against armor and helicopters, resistance tactics must be limited to small-group actions. Large concentrations will remain vulnerable to massive firepower strikes, especially from MI-24 helicopters. The few available hand-held rocket weapons have worked well against tanks and armored cars. High-velocity machine guns that can be carried by two or three men or by pack animals and quickly assembled are probably the best answer to the heavily armored gunships. Helicopter exhaust is too light for effective use of heat-seeking rockets. Wire-controlled rockets may be effective.

The resistance forces have had to use a ragtag collection of weapons, from turn-of-the-century Enfield rifles (or locally made copies) and even older weapons to the Kalishnikov automatic rifle and antitank rockets brought over by army defectors

The Shikari Valley, near Bamiyan

or seized or stolen in raids. A great miscellany of light arms is produced on the Pakistan side of the border, in such towns as Darra, where dozens of small factories compete for the trade. These producers can imitate most of the hand weapons of standard issue throughout the world. In the hands of a skilled marksman, such weapons, especially the Enfields, can be extremely effective for sniping. But locally made weapons tend to wear out quickly and the ammunition to fit them is often very costly in the rural Afghan economy. Enfield bullets were selling for $1.00 each and Kalishnikovs for $2.20 in the Pakistan market in January 1980.[55] Prices had been much higher when the Nuristanis began the struggle against the Kabul government. They suggest, however, the great financial obstacles facing the resistance in its struggle against the virtually limitless arms of the Soviets. In an economy where per capita national income is perhaps $150 per year, armament costs force the resistance to improvise within very narrow limits. Their activities in the sale of opium products on the international market are directly tied to their need to buy weapons.

Supplies of weapons capable of permitting the resistance to continue and to increase in effectiveness will require steady support from outside sources. Such support could take the form either of funds with which resistance groups could buy arms on the international market or of direct supply from friendly governments. The latter means offers the advantage of including training in the use and maintenance of weapons. To reach the resistance groups, supplies must pass through either Iran or Pakistan; the short border with China is too isolated from most theaters of fighting to serve as a useful link. The cooperation or acquiescence of Iran or Pakistan is thus crucial for an adequate flow of supplies. While contradictory statements on arms-supply policy came from both governments shortly after the invasion, each has since officially opposed the movement of weapons intended for the resistance through its territories. At Pakistan border checkpoints weapons are routinely confiscated. Yet arms sales to Afghans are not prevented. Smuggling across Afghan's borders has long since become institutionalized. Announced policies against arms movements may therefore serve primarily to avert Soviet retaliation rather than to block actual shipments. Iran and Pakistan could cut off supplies to the resistance if they imposed stringent controls. Such evidence as we have suggests that they have not clamped down totally, despite their official protestations. Much more significant, however, has been their discouragement of assistance from other governments, which has the effect of seriously limiting the amounts and kinds of supplies that can get through to the mujahidin.

Would-be suppliers have kept low profiles in their relations with the Afghan resistance. Only Egypt has openly announced a policy of support in the form of military supplies and training. Its own dependence on foreign sources for arms and Anwar Sadat's political isolation in the Muslim world restrict its ability to provide aid. It could serve, however, as a possible conduit for American aid.

The Soviet Union and the Parcham government have consistently claimed that arms supplies have been reaching the resistance from the United States, China, Saudi Arabia, Iran, Pakistan, and Egypt. Resistance spokesmen just as consistently have denied this allegation. In early March, Burhanuddin Rabani issued this statement: "While we are passing through the worst possible time for any nation, and while hundreds of thousands of Afghans are being killed by the Soviets and Afghan government, the outside world is watching the situation just like a football match. . . . [The West and sympathetic Muslim nations are acting] like unconcerned spectators, while our people are floating in their own blood."[56]

Public statements and leaks from potential suppliers have confused the situation, probably intentionally. In February Muhammad Zia-ul-Haq, president of Pakistan, was quoted as saying that his government had permitted distribution of light weapons to Afghan resistance groups.[57] At the same time the CIA was said to be smuggling arms through Pakistan.[38] Also in February, Edward Girardet, who may have covered the fighting inside Afghanistan more extensively than any other Western correspondent, found no evidence of outside training or arming of resistance groups. He also encountered Pakistani efforts to confiscate weapons from the freedom fighters.[59]

The leaking of secret documents would be the only means of resolving these contradictions. Fragmentary evidence furnished by press reports since late winter 1980 confirms Marvine Howe's conclusion in May that "only a trickle of arms is reaching the guerrillas."[60] Much of that trickle is bought with money provided quietly by the oil-rich Persian Gulf states. As we noted earlier, the Hizb-i-Islami and Gailani's group appear to be the principal beneficiaries. Hekmatyar's organization has had the money to set up a network of offices, warehouses, medical facilities, and recruiting centers in Pakistan. Its public relations activities are far better equipped, better organized, and more noticeable than those of the other groups in Pakistan. Outside support has enabled it to improve its external operations and to develop greater control over insurgent activities inside Afghanistan. Yet such improvements are marginal compared with the military capacity of the Soviet occupying forces and the need for still greater cohesion within the resistance.

The refusal of the Islamic Conference to commit itself to arming the mujahidin has been explained as a response to the resistance groups' failure to unite. This explanation ignores the fact that even though the mujahidin are not united, they have been able to harass the Russians and the Parcham government virtually everywhere and have denied them control over a large majority of the population. Their growing capacity to oppose the invading forces can be attributed to accumulated tactical and organizational experience, the capture of weapons, and a trickle of outside support. The resistance could still be decimated by a large increase in Soviet forces and greatly stepped-up attacks on rural strongholds. At the same time, the potential for an escalation of resistance activity has greatly increased; resistance groups were able to absorb far more foreign military assistance in mid-1980 than they could have done at the time of the invasion.

8

A New Era of Crisis

The use of Afghanistan as a political and military base opens an array of opportunities for expansion of Soviet trade, influence, and control in the region. If the USSR is to take advantage of such opportunities, Afghan resistance must be crushed. Its suppression would stand as an object lesson to neighboring peoples who might otherwise be tempted to try to oppose Soviet plans. The leverage gained for intimidation of neighboring states is likely to be the Soviets' most immediate gain. Intimidation can be especially effective in view of the instability of many of the region's governments and the cultural and sectarian disputes that rend its societies. Rivalries have poisoned relations among its governments. The war between Iraq and Iran is only the most glaring example of the hostility between the Muslim states of the region. There is no mechanism for collective security in the Middle East.

With the exception of India, no nation in the area has the capacity to equip and maintain a modern military force. All, including India, must depend on advanced industrial nations for sophisticated military equipment. This dependency has produced a crazy-quilt pattern of bilateral military-aid arrangements in which the United States and the USSR have played the largest roles, followed by the European industrial nations and Japan. Most Middle Eastern and South Asian governments have military contracts with two or more suppliers. The competition this situation reflects works at two levels: between suppliers, whose motives involve both profits and political influence from military sales, and between recipients, who buy or accept such weapons to defend against or threaten each other. In almost no instance have such transfers been intended or designed to defend the region as a whole.

After two decades of armament deals, the region bristles with new weapons and military forces that often serve as instruments of internal repression. Iran under the shah comes most immediately to mind, but governments topheavy with military hardware are also found in Pakistan, Bangladesh, Iraq, Syria, Saudi Arabia, Jordan, Egypt, and Israel. In each of these countries, military officers either rule directly or have great political influence. Once again, India is the only prominent exception.

Adding further to the vulnerability to these governments dependent on outside suppliers and loyal officer corps is their social and economic instability. Whether rich or poor, the weak, narrowly based governments of the Middle East—usually tribal monarchies or military dictatorships—must contend simultaneously with rapid change, conflicting demands, chronic poverty, and intrusive industrial powers that want Middle Eastern oil and strategic facilities in the region.

The Soviet Union can expect to fish much more successfully in these muddy waters if and when it pacifies Afghanistan. Having demonstrated that it can subdue the most stubborn of Muslim peoples, it would command a number of avenues for further expansion. Among the steps it might take are infiltration of minority secessionist movements; continued encouragement of Marxist opposition parties; subversion of non-Marxist elites, including military officers with grievances against their governments; the tying of economies to the Soviet bloc by selective foreign aid; and encouragement of national grievances against neighboring countries. Having established its presence at the region's doorstep and a willingness to pay the political cost of aggression in Afghanistan, the Soviet Union would have a unique opportunity to exercise ever greater influence and power.

This opportunity would come at a time when the people of the region have awakened to the profound challenge to Islam presented by modern change. The resulting ferment has affected all of the Muslim states in the region. Its most obvious manifestations have been the rise of a religious movement to political power in Iran under the Ayatollah Khomeini, the Islamic resistance movement in Afghanistan, and the attempts to purge society of Western manners and values in Iran, Pakistan, and Saudi Arabia. It has affected Muslim peoples everywhere, although in no uniform or common way. One of its features has been a heightened sense of Islamic community, as manifested in the Islamic Conference, the most comprehensive of its international forums. This emerging sense of confidence in the potency of Islam comes when its Middle Eastern heartland and adjacent South Asia are threatened by a new wave of Soviet expansionism.

Islamic ferment and the Soviet invasion present the Western world with a perplexing mix of dangers and opportunities. As its leader, the United States has attempted to meet several objectives. The Carter administration put the Soviet Union on notice that the invasion is considered a hostile act that threatens détente. It tried to assure Afghanistan's neighbors of American protection against further Soviet aggression. It tried to win a unified response to the invasion from Western Europe and Japan. It attempted to strengthen its political and quasi-military partnership with China. At home it attempted to prepare the political ground for popular acceptance of increased defense budgets. Yet, given the potential impact of the crisis, the American response has been totally inadequate. American reactions have been called "hard-line," but that characterization is applicable only to the rhetoric used to declare that business as usual with the Soviet Union will be impossible unless it withdraws from Afghanistan. The actual steps taken have been these: (1) an embargo on the export of grain from the United States to the USSR above the 8 million tons formerly agreed to by treaty; (2) an embargo on the export of high-technology goods to the Soviet Union; (3) the prohibition of Soviet fishing in U.S. territorial waters; (4) a moratorium on the opening of new U.S. and USSR consular offices; and (5) the suspension of further official cultural exchanges with the Soviet Union.

President Carter asked the U.S. Senate to delay consideration of the SALT II agreements earlier reached with the Soviet government. On January 20, 1980, he announced his opposition to American participation in the Olympic Games scheduled for Moscow in July unless Soviet troops were withdrawn from Afghanistan within a month. When the Soviets did not comply, the American government put sufficient pressure on the U.S. Olympic Committee to ensure its compliance with the boycott. All other nations were urged to join it. Supplementary measures included the reinstitution of draft registration and increases in military spending, particularly for an improved rapid-deployment capability.

The effectiveness of these reactions must be judged against their objectives. There is no evidence that they have deterred Soviet activities in Afghanistan. The economic costs to Moscow in scarcity of grain for cattle feed, interruptions in high-technology imports, and loss of access to fisheries are disputed. The USSR has found alternative sources while American farmers and some industrial suppliers have paid dearly for the loss of Soviet markets. Economic displacement has occurred; prices have risen for Soviet consumers, especially for meat and grains after an extremely poor 1980 wheat crop. The Soviet government has been embarrassed by these costs, but as in the case of most international sanctions, the Kremlin as the target government can pose as the aggrieved party, accusing the United States of trying to subject the Soviet people to unwarranted hardship. So long as Soviet citizens accept the Kremlin's pronouncement that the Red Army is helping the Afghan people, the impact of such economic sanctions can be only minimal. Perhaps even more galling to the American government than the limited effect of its embargoes has been the failure of many allied nations to enforce them. Grain and machinery have been readily available to the Soviet Union from a number of sources.

The Olympic boycott was intended to be a symbolic act of solidarity against aggression. As an invader the Soviet Union was to be treated as a pariah, not a host. The impact of the boycott was to be psychological, with political implications. Such intangibles are nearly impossible to assess. Much of the effect was lost when most Western European teams attended, yet the absence of the United States, Japan, China, West Germany, and several smaller nations was too obvious to be overlooked. In effect the games became a contest within the Soviet bloc, with a few medals won by outsiders. The loss of universality was unmistakable. But even if a pall hung over the event for the Soviet people, it is unlikely to have much political effect on them unless the war for Afghanistan goes badly. Then some Russians may recall the embarrassment of the boycott. If pacification is a success, the government and the Soviet army can claim credit as statesmen and heroes, and the doubts raised by the boycott will be forgotten.

In sum, then, the measures taken by the United States may have irritated and certainly have alienated the Soviet Union, but they have produced no substantial effect on the situation created by the invasion. In fact, their superficiality doomed them to failure from the beginning. The American response was superficial because it was not rooted in the realities triggered by the invasion. Recognition of this fact was one of the reasons for the reluctance of its allies to sacrifice the benefits of amicable relations with Moscow for such a futile course of action.

The primary inadequacy of American policy lay in the fact that it immediately conceded Afghanistan. Carter conveyed that concession even in his strongest denunciations of the invasion. In the first hours Carter accused the Soviets of "blatant violation of the accepted rules of international behavior." His hotline message to Brezhnev warned of "serious consequences" if the Soviets did not withdraw. In a television interview on December 31, 1979, Carter exclaimed that the Afghan crisis was the most serious since World War II and that it had changed his thinking about the Soviet leadership. The consequences anticipated by these threatening statements were the boycott and embargo actions described above and the general chilling of U.S. relations with the Kremlin, particularly over the fate of SALT II.

Despite his rhetoric, the president made it clear in his State of the Union address on January 23, 1980, that the United States would take no direct action to dislodge the Soviets from Afghanistan. Instead he drew the line at the Persian Gulf. A Soviet attack on the gulf "would be repelled by the use of any means necessary, including military force." No definition of the Persian Gulf "region" was furnished, but Carter's own policies made it clear that Afghanistan was considered to lie beyond it. By concentrating on indirect pressure against the Soviets, the United States tacitly admitted that it does not have the physical means to force the Soviets to withdraw their troops.

Part of America's difficulty lies, of course, in the great logistical and geostrategic disadvantages inherent in Aghanistan's location. The Russians are neighbors, the Americans are not. This disadvantage could be offset only by strong ties to governments in the region that feared Soviet aggression toward themselves. The invasion has demonstrated how fragile and unreliable such ties are.

While all of the Middle Eastern nations save Syria and South Yemen condemned the invasion, only Egypt and Israel rushed to embrace the United States as an ally. The reasons for this reluctance are complex and variable. Essentially, they involve deep suspicions about American motives and capabilities. Governments friendly to the United States (Saudi Arabia, Jordan, Pakistan) worried that close military cooperation might weaken domestic support and inflame relations with their neighbors. Unfriendly governments—Iran, Iraq, Syria—pointed to the line drawn by Carter at the Persian Gulf as a sign of American interference in their region. As a result, no viable diplomatic foundation for a structure of collective security has been created. It was this lack of a political base that forced the U.S. government to resort to symbols and gestures instead of concrete steps to shore up regional defenses.

An effective response was made more difficult by decisions that led to an unspoken conclusion that Afghanistan had already fallen into the Soviet camp. When Afghan Marxists seized power in April 1978, the international community implicitly accepted the changed situation. There were no diplomatic reactions to Moscow's declaration that Afghanistan had joined the Socialist bloc. International acquiesence in 1978 made opposition to the invasion in 1979 all the more difficult.

When Afghan Marxists seized power, proclaimed a socialist state, and inflamed the population with the sudden imposition of radical reforms, America's policy was limited to preserving ongoing but diminishing aid programs and maintaining its diplomatic status in Kabul. Not until Ambassador Adolph Dubs was killed did the U.S. government take a disapproving stand against the Marxist regime. But by that time the United States no longer had any means of influencing the situation in Afghanistan. Its influence through aid had come to a dead end. Open hostility toward the Marxist regime in Kabul would only have forced it even further into Moscow's embrace. At the same time, America's continued willingness to recognize and to aid the Kabul Marxists powerfully implied acceptance of a new political situation saturated by Soviet influence. Even after Dubs's murder had frozen Washington-Kabul relations, American protests against growing Soviet involvement were lodged in mild terms.

In August 1979 Zbigniew Brzezinski, Carter's national security adviser and his administration's most outspoken opponent of Soviet expansionism, declared the Middle East to be a "vital strategic zone" but avoided mentioning the Soviet Union by name when warning that "we expect others . . . to abstain from intervention and from efforts to impose alien doctrines on deeply religious and nationally conscious peoples."[1] This unpointed rumble was followed the next month by testimony from Harold Saunders, secretary of state for Near East and South Asian affairs, that the United States was "especially disturbed by the growing involvement of the Soviet Union in Afghanistan affairs." This statement came ten months after the Kabul government had signed a friendship treaty with the Soviet Union which essentially made Afghanistan a political, economic, and military extension of the socialist bloc. Saunders claimed that the United States would "monitor" Soviet military involvement in Afghanistan and had "repeatedly impressed on the Soviet government the danger of more direct involvement in the fighting in Afghanistan."[2]

American policy was caught between the Soviet might and the Afghan resistance. It conceded Soviet dominance by not offering encouragement to Afghans fighting against it. This passive posture signaled an American unwillingness to intervene further. Regardless of expressions of "deep concern" at threats to Afghanistan's integrity, Washington offered no evidence that it was prepared to prevent a Soviet military takeover.

This lack of preparation was the result of policy failures that extended to most of the Middle East and South Asia. Support of Israel and a generalized fear of communist expansion governed American policy toward the region as a whole until the oil embargo imposed by the Arab producers in 1973 brought a sudden awakening to the economic importance of the region. Events since then have only dramatized the urgency of more comprehensive, balanced, and precise approaches to the region.

By the time of the Soviet invasion of Afghanistan, U.S. influence in the region had shrunk alarmingly. By focusing virtually all of its diplomatic resources on a search for a solution to the Arab-Israeli conflict through the Camp David accords between Egypt and Israel, the United States had alienated almost all of the Arab states. Saudi Arabia, with its fear of communism and possible internal revolt, remained ambivalent, but resented American commitments to Israel.

The nations of South Asia were also alienated. Pakistan no longer trusted America to support it in its ongoing conflict with India. Indo-American relations remained sour primarily because of accumulated disagreements over India's increasingly obvious role as a major regional power.

American impotence in the region at the time of the invasion was epitomized by the total impasse with Iran following the seizure of American embassy personnel as hostages on November 4, 1979. This act brought sharply into focus the volatile processes working in the region and the inadequacy of American policy. Iran had become immersed in an elemental revolution after the fall of Muhammad Reza Shah in January 1979. For influence in the Persian Gulf the United States had relied heavily on an unpopular, repressive regime. Adjustment to the new and rapidly fluctuating situation in Iran was proving to be painful and difficult. In place of a partner in a political/military/economic alliance based on the shah's willingness to defend the region in return for American support, Iran was now a nation in chaos, led by religious zealots who blamed the United States for the shah's regime. The collapse of American-Iranian relations was far more than the rupture of an alliance of mutual convenience. It exposed the great distance between the social and cultural realities even in one of the richest and most "developed" nations of the region and American understanding of the forces at work. At the core of the process was the regenerative energy of Islam, calling on Muslims to reconcile the tenets of their faith with the often clashing demands of modern change. Ignoring specialists in and out of government who warned of revolutionary ferment based on Islamic revival (with varying admixtures of Western ideas, from liberalism to Marxism), American policy clung to an established relationship with an entrenched ruler.

It has been Islamic revivalism, not communism, that has undercut the American position in the Middle East, including Pakistan. The resulting weakness further assured the Soviets that American protest against intervention in Afghanistan could be disregarded.

Yet the Islamic revival also presented an obstacle to Soviet expansionism. While some of the new Islamic champions—most notably Muammar Khadafy of Libya—claim to combine socialism with Islamic fundamentalism, most Islamic spokesmen opposed Marxism to varying degrees for varying reasons. Islam itself has thus stood as a barrier to Soviet influence and penetration in most parts of the region. Yet the divisive character of the ferment greatly weakened the prospects for effective unity against outside pressure. The Islamic revolution in Iran brought new disputes with its neighbors and rekindled old ones. Border claims and charges of mistreatment of minorities exploded into war with Iraq. Historic claims to Bahrain brought cries of dismay not only from its amir but from Saudi Arabia and the other small oil states. Export of the revolution from Shia Iran sat poorly with the surrounding states, which are predominantly

Sunni. Khadafy's expansive claims to lead a new Islamic order, promoted largely by the financing of opposition and terrorist groups within other Muslim countries, have also aroused hostility and fear. The revival has generated great energy in Islamic politics, but these divisions and disagreements threaten to dissipate its impact. Soviet calculations of the response of the Muslim community to the invasion seem to have been realistic. Nearly universal protest and two Islamic conferences have not shaken the Soviet hold on Afghanistan.

At an extraordinary meeting of the Islamic Conference at Islamabad, Pakistan, in January 1980, the invasion was labeled aggression and condemned. A consensus resolution demanded complete withdrawal of Soviet troops, suspended the Kabul government from the conference itself, and called on member states to boycott the summer Olympic Games in Moscow.[4] Muslim states were urged to "affirm their solidarity with the Afghan people in their just struggle to safeguard their faith, national independence and territorial integrity." All nations were asked to provide relief assistance to Afghan refugees. Provision was made to collect funds to aid the Afghan resistance. (See Appendix 1, clause 9.) The secretary of the conference was authorized to receive contributions from member states for disbursement for purposes left unspecified.

Even the PLO and governments closely allied to the Soviet Union—Libya, Algeria, Iraq—joined in this clear denunciation of the invasion. But four months later the Muslim stand was softened and its focus blurred by competing concerns over Israel and the United States. Condemnation of the Soviet invasion and insistence on the withdrawal of Soviet troops were retained, the right of the Afghan people to govern themselves was reaffirmed, but no call was made to support them in their struggle. Instead, the conference instructed a committee to seek a political solution. This committee of three, composed of Iran's and Pakistan's foreign ministers and the secretary general of the Islamic Conference, was to negotiate with the Soviet Union, the Kabul government, and representatives of the Afghan resistance. (See Appendix 2.) The impact of the earlier resolution was blunted. The Islamic world no longer hinted at assistance to Afghan freedom fighters. The previous resolution had not brought about a Soviet withdrawal. Instead, both superpowers were now active in the region. In late April the United States had staged a raid in an unsuccessful attempt to rescue the hostages in Iran. The American military presence had been greatly increased, particularly through deployment of the U.S. Navy. Diplomatic efforts were being made to set up American bases in or near the Persian Gulf. Muslim sensitivity to any outside intervention gave the pro-Soviet spokesmen at the second conference an opportunity to divert its focus from the Russians. Accordingly, the conference was induced to condemn Israeli occupation of the West Bank, American meddling, and Egyptian apostasy along with Soviet aggression.

This inclination to soften the response to the invasion was not restricted to Third World governments. In late February, Prime Minister Margaret Thatcher's British government suggested Afghan "neutralization" as a solution. Other NATO powers took up this approach and attempted to interest the Soviets and Americans in it. Moscow courted the envoys who came to discuss the idea, but claimed that Afghanistan had a sovereign government that was already a member of the nonaligned bloc and that Soviet military presence there would cease as soon as Americans and their allies stopped interfering in the country. Washington was also unreceptive. The presence of Soviet troops could not be squared with credible "neutrality." Tass's conclusion that a neutrality scheme was "illogical" was perhaps an unintendedly apt epitaph for the proposal. Neutrality had been the cornerstone of Afghanistan's foreign relations before the home-grown Marxists and Soviet invaders had changed them. To suggest it return to such a posture was either fatuous nonsense, based on an assumption that the Soviets were now willing to give up their hold over the country, or a diplomatic device to disguise Soviet control by pretending that the Kabul government was sovereign and nonaligned. Neither position was tenable. The Soviet Union refused to withdraw, the United States refused to accept a pretense of neutrality.

200

European critics of American responses to the invasion made telling points in defense of their own soft reactions. They complained that Washington overreacted. They claimed that the Soviets were merely straightening out a struggle between Afghan Marxists; that the United States sounded an unnecessary alarm over the threat to Persian Gulf oil; that it rushed into embargoes and boycotts without real consultations with other countries; that its Middle East policies were so weighted toward the Arab-Israeli dispute that Muslim nations rejected Western help for regional defense; in sum, that the invasion of Afghanistan was not an issue vital enough to disturb East-West détente. Such a line of argument permitted most Western European governments to continue and even to increase their trade in high-technology goods with Moscow at the expense of American exporters.

By the summer of 1980 no nation or bloc of nations had taken an effective position against the invasion. The United States groped for bases in the Middle East and debated how to expand its military strength. It had failed to encourage or to share in the creation of a collective security system for the nations of South and West Asia. Divided and suspicious of each other, these nations backed off from a forceful condemnation of the invasion of a brother Muslim nation. European industrial nations, critically dependent on Middle Eastern oil, acted to put the Afghan crisis behind them.

World response has thus been uneven, halting, and generally timid. It has obviously failed to dislodge the Soviet army. This failure to repel or even seriously to punish aggression has been accompanied by a serious deterioration in Soviet-American relations which threatens the whole structure of peace through mutual restraint and deterrence. The crisis has become a classic demonstration of the delicacy of the international order. Progress in arms control has been stalled, perhaps indefinitely. Hardliners in both superpowers have increased their influence, forcing their more accommodating political rivals to show more toughness. The soured American public mood following the invasion undoubtedly contributed to Carter's defeat by Ronald Reagan in the national elections of 1980. Military budgets are expanding accordingly. Resources available for attacks on the global problems of food, energy, environmental decay, and social dislocation will correspondingly diminish. Suspicion has replaced cautious optimism about the gradual relaxation of interbloc tensions. The turn of a decade has brought the beginning of a new and threatening era.

For Americans the resulting sense of futility, coupled with continuing anger over Iran's seizure of hostages and dismay over the decline of U.S. influence on global events, has produced a dangerously charged political climate. Isolationist tendencies evident since the Vietnam War could degenerate into a bitter jingoism as political leaders call for ever tougher military solutions to alleged threats to security.

None of the overt American responses to the crisis was focused on Afghanistan itself. They had no direct application to the actual struggle between Afghans and Soviets. Minimal attention has been paid to a million refugees who have fled to Iran and Pakistan. No official encouragement has been given to the resistance groups. Any military aid they have received has been given covertly, and it has been too small to affect the fighting more than a year after the invasion. Despite its strident rhetoric about the seriousness of the crisis, the American government even failed to beam radio transmissions to Afghanistan. Six months after the invasion no one had been hired by Voice of America to broadcast to Afghanistan. While massive shifts in global positions went on, no specific policies or actions were devised to deal with the ongoing crisis that caused them.

Such actions as have been attempted were hastily and poorly carried out. An offer of arms was made to Pakistan without adequate study of the deployment of its forces or its political capacity to absorb sudden military aid. No systematic attempt was made to encourage the cooperation of India in a plausible scheme for defense of the subcontinent. Attempts to obtain naval facilities and supply bases for future rapid-deployment missions in the Persian Gulf ignored the internal stress generated by foreign bases and the impossibility of matching the Soviet Union's ability to send forces into an area immediately adjacent to its borders. It remains to be seen whether the agreement on use by the United States of Ports in Kenya, Somalia, and Oman will be workable or will be subject to conditions and pressures that cancel out their value. Meanwhile, friendly governments, most notably Saudi Arabia, have made it clear that they want no American forces on their soil.

These attempts to create a military capacity in the Indian Ocean and the Middle East have also induced nonaligned or openly hostile governments to harden their positions to virtually a pox-on-both-their-houses stance vis-à-vis the United States and the USSR. Iraq, Iran, and India, whatever their differences, have clearly expressed their dislike of American bases in the region. Consequently, the Carter administration's initiatives following the invasion have had a Catch-22 effect. The stronger the American military presence becomes, the harder it becomes to win cooperation from the very nations whose security is involved. Regional governments are forced into what they see as a Hobson's choice between superpowers when they prefer to keep out both. The present U.S. policy limits the possibility of a collective defense of the region based on indigenous military and diplomatic arrangements. By muscling in without consideration of the political realities, American military policy is very likely to weaken the prospects for an eventual regional response to further Soviet aggression.

This tendency of American policy to thwart American objectives is especially damaging in the cases of Israel and India. During the thirty-two years that the United States has supported Israel against the Arab refusal to accept its existence as a state, it has become increasingly difficult to separate the essentials of Israel's security from the compulsions of internal Israeli and American politics. One consequence, crucial for the American position throughout the region, has been the tendency to assess relationships with other countries on the basis of their effect on Israel. One of the attractions of the shah of Iran was his willingness to supply oil to Israel and to lend it diplomatic support. The United States' ability to achieve a considerable degree of cooperation with Saudi Arabia is based not only on Riyadh's willingness to be America's major source of oil, but also on the restraint it exercises in opposing Israel. The costs to the United States of the failure to reconcile the Arabs and the Israelis have been high, and they increase as the capacity for Soviet intervention grows. An obsession with one nation to the exclusion of all others has so unbalanced the American role in the region that few secure roots of cooperation and mutual interest have taken hold. The Afghan crisis has demonstrated that a formula for settlement of the Palestinian question on a basis acceptable to most Arab states is a sine qua non for an effective American role in the Middle East. Without it, Muslim leaders will continue to be as concerned with Israel as a wedge of American intervention as they are with possible Soviet aggression. Only when Israel is accepted as a nonthreatening neighbor can U.S.–Middle East policy be balanced to conform to the complexity and importance of this region.

America's influence and options in the region are also serious-ly hampered by its almost total failure to develop a satisfactory understanding with India on matters of regional security. Vex-ing as Indian actions and criticisms of the United States have been in the past, most of the responsibility for unsatisfactory relations must be attributed to America's misconception of India as a nation. Despite the definitive result of the Bangladesh war of 1971, the United States has failed to recognize India as the dominant power in South Asia and as one of the major arbiters of the future of the Indian Ocean region and Asia as a whole. It has refused to take India seriously, continuing to see it as a weak, have-not nation, unstable internally and dependent on others for survival. By operating on such a false premise, the American regional policy has consistently generated India's hostility since Washington began to ship arms to Pakistan in 1954. A quarter-century of subsequent friction almost inevitably prevented the two nations from agreeing on the meaning of the Soviet move into Afghanistan and from finding a mutually agreeable form of response. Indian and American policy have been at odds on every major facet of the crisis. Indian spokesmen have criticized the Soviet action but refrain from calling it an invasion. They accept the allegation that outside interference provoked the Russians to move in. India abstained on the U.N. General Assembly resolution to condemn the invasion. While expressing concern over the Soviet presence, it recognized the new Parcham government and makes plain the continuity of friendly relations with Moscow. Presumably in return for this attitude, India was offered $1.5 billion worth of new military aid by the USSR. India was, of course, well represented at the Moscow Olympics.

In addition to undermining American opposition to the invasion, Indian hostility played a large role in Pakistan's decision to refuse American military aid. Indira Gandhi's new government further alienated Washington when it offered to expand trade with Iran in goods embargoed by the United States.

On almost every pressing global issue these two great democracies are at odds. The Soviet invasion graphically demonstrates how damaging this impasse has become. India has the only large, thoroughly professional, nonpolitical, and internally trained armed forces in the Indian Ocean basin. Since its defeat in a limited mountain war by China in 1962, India has built a capacity to wage conventional modern war which is at least 75 percent self-sufficient. No other nation in South or West Asia has a remotely comparable military capability.

By ignoring India's political stability and military sophistication, the United States has lost the opportunity to base its regional policy on cooperation with its permanently dominant power. Consequently, every American initiative must struggle uphill against the resentment and hostility of a government that expects to be taken seriously.

Largely in default of an accommodative American policy and prodded by its rivalry with China, India has turned to the Soviet Union for defense assistance and formal treaty agreements to ensure its security. Indian leaders can hardly have missed the implications of armed Soviet aggression in the direction of the subcontinent, but lacking a credible alternative to continued

205

cooperation with the Soviet Union, they have not been in a position to make the radical adjustments that open hostility to the invasion would require.

Cooperation between India and the United States may be difficult to achieve, but the potential benefits for both would make the attempt worthwhile. The basic goals of both countries overlap considerably, especially for South Asia as a whole: peaceful stability, integrity of the existing states, unimpaired movement of goods (especially for petroleum consumers), acceleration of economic development, and encouragement of open democratic political systems. Effective multilateral cooperation to achieve these ends requires American willingness to refrain from unilateral attempts to shape interstate relations within the region to its own convenience. For its part, India must admit the need to defend its region from demonstrated aggression from the north. It will take an extraordinary diplomatic effort by both sides to make the required changes in attitude and habit.

Despite the failure of the international community to halt Soviet aggression, the USSR has so far gained little from the invasion. Yet it is the only protagonist that has the ability to resolve the crisis to its own satisfaction. If it is willing to pay the costs, it can destroy the Afghan opposition by perfecting counterinsurgency techniques, by forcing the movement and resettlement of large sections of the population (either as refugees or as inmates of fortified villages or camps), and by sharply increasing the size of its military forces inside Afghanistan. Without substantial outside support to offset such an escalation, the resistance groups would be forced to retreat into remote, largely uninhabitable regions or across the Iranian and Pakistani borders. The latter development would almost certainly bring about increasingly effective Soviet pressure on those states to disarm and intern the mujahidin. At that point the resistance would find itself hopelessly isolated. The Muslim community and the Western bloc could console themselves with the thought that they had made gestures of protest against an invasion that the Afghans and their sympathizers could not prevent. Having already conceded Afghanistan to the USSR, they would be prepared to accept complete suppression of the resistance as inevitable.

Despite its claims of outside intervention, the Soviet government has been confident that no other power could interfere. Such interference would have risked the whole fabric of global peace. The feeble reactions to the invasion made it clear that no other nation considers Afghanistan's independence to be worth the gamble. Such caution might have been prudent if the danger posed by the invasion could be restricted to Afghanistan alone. In fact, there is little chance that it can be limited to Afghanistan. The initiative that the Soviets can gain from a conquest of Afghanistan is virtually certain to expose the Persian Gulf region to increasingly effective political penetration. Once the Afghan resistance is silenced, the governments and political groups in the region can be expected to rush to make peace with the USSR. The Soviet government will then have no need to resort to military moves to gain dominance over the region. The consequences for the global order and the international petroleum market are incalculable; at the very least they will be severely damaging to the United States, Western Europe, and Japan.

Continuing resistance by the Afghan mujahidin is the only factor actively working against this scenario. Unless or until the resistance is crushed, the Russians confront serious obstacles. Continued fighting in Afghanistan will mean the further stirring of Muslim hostility and growing complaints by the Soviets themselves about the costs and casualties and the embarrassing spectacle of a massive army with modern equipment trying to annihilate a poorly armed people's movement. The United States, the nations of South Asia, and all countries dependent on oil from the Persian Gulf therefore have a vital stake in the mujahidin of Afghanistan. In them lies the possibility of denying to the Soviet Union the opportunity to use Afghanistan as a base for expansion into the Middle East.

This possibility has come as a surprise to everyone except the Afghans. At the time of the invasion a quick Soviet conquest was expected. Even American military observers publicly expressed grudging respect for the effectiveness of the planning and execution of the Soviet move.[3] The international community equated the presence of six Red Army divisions with the effective occupation of the country. These conclusions were wrong because the Afghan mujahidin were determined to resist and the Russians were unprepared to deal with resourceful guerrilla opponents. The outside world conceded Afghanistan prematurely. Within five months it was clear that the resistance had not been destroyed; it was spreading and becoming stronger. Unfortunately, the opportunity thus offered the world community to reassess the situation has not been taken. The policies of Western and Muslim nations remain frozen to their original miscalculations. Continuing Afghan resistance has bought time for them to adjust and react; the mujahidin have opened a window in time that might be used to transform the situation. The United States still has an opportunity to work with the nations of the region to help the freedom fighters to retrieve their country.

To be effective, an American response must come soon and it must be adept. It must enlist the cooperation of the Muslim nations of the region and the acquiescence of India. The United States must provide assistance to the Afghan resistance on a dependable, long-term basis. Such support should and can be designed to promote greater integration of the mujahid forces inside Afghanistan and to resolve the divisions among their political leaders. Total unity, however, does not have to be a precondition for outside support. Successes already achieved by the mujahidin refute the argument that resistance cannot succeed without unity. The first issue before the Afghan resistance is not unity, but the survival of the national liberation effort.

The resistance forces can be expected to face improved and increasingly determined efforts to destroy them. As the Soviets learn from their mistakes, they will adapt their command structure and their tactics to fit Afghan conditions. They can also be expected to use divide-and-rule tactics aimed especially at separating the larger minorities from the Pushtuns. Altogether, the Soviets' capability to divide or destroy Afghan opposition will grow. Any chance of their abandonment of their Afghan adventure therefore requires a marked increase in the ability of the resistance to survive and carry on its struggle.

Standing alone against massively superior Soviet forces, the resistance has little hope of holding out indefinitely. It might be able to continue raids in remote areas, but in a war of attrition the Soviet occupation army could eventually solidify control over all of the most productive and populated rural regions. To do so the Kremlin will need to increase its ground forces to as many as 300,000 plus the required support units.

The increased effectiveness of the mujahidin in the summer of 1980 suggests that timely outside assistance could help vitally in preventing the Russians from crushing them by means of large reinforcements and improved tactics. The Kremlin must weigh the very large economic, political, military, and morale costs of expanding its war in Afghanistan. Its pacification and opportunities for expansion in the Middle East must be balanced against the Soviet Union's heavy commitments to defense of its border with China, to the preservation of its control over Eastern Europe, to continued support of Vietnamese aggression in Southeast Asia, and to satisfaction of the growing material demands of its own population. A minimum level of amity and trade with the West, Japan, and Middle Eastern nations is an essential component of such calculations. For these reasons a virtual all-out war in Afghanistan could appear to the Soviet government to entail unacceptable risk. Its hesitation to escalate the war might be increased if the Kremlin were convinced that the resistance movement was assured of substantial outside aid. The prospect of mutual escalation could induce the Soviets to give serious consideration to a formula for withdrawal behind some face-saving device. If they were confident that the mujahidin were not going to receive help, the Soviets certainly would have less incentive to consider withdrawal.

Soviet uncertainty over developments in Afghanistan was evident in the shifting of units, new command arrangements, and testing of new tactics late in the summer of 1980. This activity suggests that time is of the essence if the resistance groups are to be reorganized and reequipped before the Soviet command can multiply its forces and perfect its tactics. For the mujahidin, survival itself may eventually bring victory. Should Soviet reinforcements fail to destroy the resistance, Moscow may again pause to consider a political compromise consistent with Afghan independence.

Military assistance could therefore play a pivotal part in determining the outcome of the war. Its costs in military equipment need not be large; they could be modest compared with Soviet assistance to Hanoi during the Vietnam War. The equipment involved would necessarily be restricted to light infantry weapons, including human- or animal-carried antitank and anti-helicopter armament, basic medical supplies, and portable communications gear. From the point of view of cost alone, almost any of Afghanistan's Muslim neighbors could provide enough support to make a significant difference in the effectiveness of mujahid efforts. Matériel, not foreign manpower, is essential.

Politics provides a more serious obstacle. Significant amounts of aid can reach the resistance only through Iran or Pakistan. Both will be reluctant to anger the Soviet Union by supplying or permitting aid to reach the resistance unless they are convinced that such a course would put them in no danger. Both governments suffer from severe internal and foreign impediments to the taking of bold steps contrary to Soviet interests. The Iranian revolution has yet to reach a stage where it can support a strong government; popular support for Pakistan's third martial-law regime remains narrow and uncertain. No solution has been found to Pakistan's obsessive concern over threats to its security from India; Iran under Shia revivalism has poor relations with almost all of its neighbors. The vulnerability of these two states can be compensated for only by joint regional action clearly directed at enhancing their security. The Soviet invasion has provided a powerful stimulus in this direction, but the reaction has not so far been strong enough to overcome the mutual suspicions that divide the region. Rivalries between Muslim governments are not the only obstacle; there is also a vital need to include China in the defense of South Asia, but China's involvement requires a difficult reconcilation with India.

Cooperation among Iran, Pakistan, and their neighbors is based on the common political front formed by the Islamic Conference against the Soviet invasion. By midsummer 1980 the negotiating committee of the conference had met with representatives of the Afghan resistance in Switzerland. The committee's initial goal continued to be to induce the Afghans to unite into one political movement. The conference members place great stress on Afghan unity. The war between Iraq and Iran demonstrates that there is an even greater need for unity among the Muslim nations themselves. Neither Iran nor Pakistan should be expected to confront the Soviet Union over Afghanistan alone. The lack of regional backing was a major reason for Pakistan's refusal of American military aid shortly after the invasion.

It is in connection with this crucial need for Muslim unity that the United States—with appropriate modifications in policy—could play an important catalytic role. By offering to supply military and medical equipment *at the request* of the Islamic Conference or some other agency that might be established to conduct collective regional defense, the United States could act as a counterforce against Soviet encroachment without intruding its own military forces directly into the region. Such an approach could enhance the security of the region without requiring the establishment of American bases, which almost all states of the region fear as destabilizing intrusions. A great deal of innovative diplomacy would be required to demonstrate an American willingness to support rather than to lead or dominate a coalition of nations banded together for their own benefit.

Solutions to the problems of Israel's status and the impasse between the United States and Iran are only two of the many thorny barriers that must be breached if a firm foundation is to be laid for such cooperation. The provision of aid to the Afghan resistance could be a superb demonstration that such cooperation is possible on a matter of vital interest to the nations of the region. It would enable the United States to prove its bona fides as a friend rather than an imperialist predator. In restricting its role to providing equipment and medical aid, the United States could keep its profile low while making a substantial contribution. For American participation to be acceptable to governments of the region, the U.S. government must be willing to turn over control of the material it provides to a joint regional authority.

An arrangement of this sort risks almost nothing save the cost of the equipment provided. It would demonstrate American willingness to leave the affairs of the region in the hands of its own governments. It would dramatize the common concern of all parties with the threat of further Soviet expansion. It could provide a model for future American relations with the region.

A commitment to assist the mujahidin through regional cooperation would be far more effective than any of the self-limiting gestures attempted by the Carter administration. Movement toward a program of aid could be developed step by step, in such a way that the Soviets were given ample notice and thus a chance to consider their responses to the increasing pressure that a united stand behind the resistance forces could exert.

As a first step, a marked increase in American contributions for relief of the more than 1.5 million Afghan refugees in Pakistan and Iran might be announced. Arrangements for such contributions could be worked out with the United Nations Relief Agency and the Pakistani government without disturbing India and other states in the region. Cooperation with Iran would, of course, be more difficult. Its government is unstable, and the release of the American hostages was only the first step in the settlement of the disputes between the United States and Iran.

As a second step, after consultation with regional governments the United States could announce its willingness to deal with an Afghan government in exile. This move could induce the Peshawar groups to join with the Momaselu Jirgah, which is the most representative of the resistance groups fighting inside Afghanistan. Movement in this direction would open up a number of opportunities to prod the Kremlin into reconsidering its position. It could be made aware beforehand of American interests in a government in exile. Discussion of the stages of development leading to the formation of such a government could be noisy enough for the Soviets to overhear. Such discussion could include debate and consultation over recognition of an exile government and over preparations for the provision of aid to the resistance. Such developments can be expected to have far greater impact on Soviet policy than any international action since the invasion was condemned by the General Assembly of the United Nations.

These indications of support for the resistance could be combined with the first stage of supplying or greatly expanding the supply (if there has been clandestine support) of military equipment for the mujahidin. These steps can be taken only after Pakistan, at least, agrees to the arrangements on the basis of regional assent and support. Extremely important in this regard would be reassurance to India that the supplies provided would be suitable for guerrilla warfare only and therefore that their delivery through Pakistan would present no material threat to India. Advance warning might also profitably be given the Soviets. They would thus have further opportunity to contemplate their position rather than being forced to react to a sudden fait accompli. Should they respond negatively, there would be no reason to keep the aid covert. Since the supplies would be transferred by regional governments to the resistance, American involvement, openly avowed, could greatly improve the standing of the United States in the region and beyond.

From that point on, the joint assistance effort would have to be adjusted to meet changing military and political circumstances. Most important, it would have to be conducted in a manner that above all else would be sensitive to the needs of the resistance forces and their progress toward unity.

The advantages of such a course far outweigh their costs and risks. It permits the United States to support a cause popular with almost all peoples of Asia and the Third World without becoming directly involved in the fighting itself. It can serve as a means of helping the forces of Islamic unity rally to the defense of fellow Muslims. In that respect it would, for the first time, place the United States squarely in support of the Islamic revival. In this fashion it can make clear that American interests in South and West Asia are not purely intrusive or selfish. By acting to help a beleaguered people regain its independence, American policy would once again be championing the cause of national liberation. Self-determination for Afghanistan's neighbors can be ensured only if they develop a common defense against all outside powers. In committing itself to respect such a collective arrangement, the United States can show that it accepts cooperation without demanding the right to dominate.

A policy that develops in this direction cannot ensure the liberation of Afghanistan. That result must depend primarily on Soviet perceptions and Afghan courage. Such a policy cannot guarantee the return of a moderate, democratic, or development-oriented government in Afghanistan should the Russians leave. It does offer a possibility that people courageous enough to fight a neighboring superpower may have a chance to govern themselves by their own lights. In a world of nations such a cause should be sufficient to bring all free governments to their side.

Whatever the odds against them, the mujahidin can be expected to seek martyrdom or victory. Many on both sides will be robbed of life by the lethal futilities of war. The loss may perhaps have been expressed best by a Soviet paratrooper who died before spring arrived in Afghanistan:

I am going away, said the lad to her through his grief,
Not for a long time.
Wait for me and I will return.

He went off, never met up with
His first spring. He came home
In a soldier's metal coffin.

He did not live beyond the hour before dawn.
He fell on his chest and closed up the ground with his wounds,
He fell on his chest not during war but in peace,
When spring ignites the stars of love for us.

Mother sobs and father
Stands like a shadow.
For them he was just a very young man.

And how many of them, who have not
Yet made the first step in life
Have come home in a soldier's metal coffin?

And once, when he went walking with his girl,
He gave her flowers
And played a song for her on his guitar,
And even in the instant when the snow grew stale, when the thaw came,
He wrote down in blood the name of that little girl.

The wind scattered the flurrying snow above the grave.
That girl has gone off with another lad,
That girl who promised, "I will wait."
The snow has thawed, the name has disappeared with it.

Appendix 1

Resolutions on Afghanistan Adopted January 28, 1980, at the Extraordinary Meeting of the Foreign Ministers of the Islamic Conference

AFFIRMING that the Soviet occupation of Afghanistan constitutes a violation of its independence, and aggression against the liberty of its people and a flagrant violation of all international covenants and norms, as well as a serious threat to peace and security in the region and throughout the world, [the First Extraordinary Session of the Islamic Foreign Ministers]

1. CONDEMNS the Soviet military aggression against the Afghan people, denounces and deplores it as a flagrant violation of international laws, covenants, and norms, primarily the Charter of the United Nations, which condemned this aggression in its Resolution No. ES-6/2 of 14 January 1980, and the charter of the Organization of the Islamic Conference, and calls upon all peoples and governments throughout the world to persist in condemning this aggression and denouncing it as an aggression against human rights and a violation of the freedoms of people, which cannot be ignored;

2. DEMANDS the immediate and unconditional withdrawal of all Soviet troops stationed on Afghan territories, and reiterates that Soviet troops should refrain from acts of oppression and tyranny against the Afghan people and their struggling sons until the departure of the last Soviet soldier from Afghan terri-

From *New York Times*, January 30, 1980, p. A13. Official English text: Reuters.

tory, and urges all countries and peoples to secure the Soviet withdrawal through all possible means;

3. SUSPENDS the membership of Afghanistan in the Organization of the Islamic Conference;

4. INVITES the member states to withhold recognition to the illegal regime in Afghanistan and sever diplomatic relations with that country until the complete withdrawal of Soviet troops from Afghanistan;

5. CALLS UPON all member states to stop all aid and all forms of assistance given to the present regime of Afghanistan by member states;

6. URGES all states and people throughout the world to support the Afghan people and provide assistance and succor to the refugees whom aggression has driven away from their homes;

7. RECOMMENDS to all member states to affirm their solidarity with the Afghan people in their just struggle to safeguard their faith, national independence, and territorial integrity and to recover their right to determine their destiny;

8. SOLEMNLY DECLARES its complete solidarity with the Islamic countries neighboring Afghanistan against any threat to their security and well-being and calls upon states of the Islamic Conference to resolutely support and extend all possible cooperation to these countries in their efforts to fully safeguard their sovereignty, national independence, and territorial integrity;

9. AUTHORIZES the secretary to receive contributions from member states, organizations, and individuals and to disperse the amounts to the authorities concerned on the recommendations of a committee of three member states to be established by him in consultation with the states concerned;

10. CALLS UPON member states to envisage through appropriate bodies the nonparticipation in Olympic Games being held in Moscow in July 1980 until the Soviet Union, in compliance with the call of the U.N. General Assembly and Islamic Conference, withdraws all its troops forthwith from Afghanistan.

Appendix 2

Resolutions on Afghanistan Adopted May 22, 1980, by the Conference of Islamic Foreign Ministers

EXPRESSING its deep conviction that termination of Soviet military intervention in Afghanistan and respect for the political independence, sovereignty, and nonaligned status of Afghanistan and for the inalienable national right of the Afghan people to choose their own political and socio-economic system and form of government without outside interference or coercion are imperative for bringing about conditions of peace and stability in the region and for defusing current international tensions;

SERIOUSLY CONCERNED at the sufferings of the Afghan people and at the continuing influx of Afghan refugees into Pakistan and Iran;

DEEPLY CONSCIOUS of the objective enshrined in the charter of the Islamic Conference requiring the member states to strengthen the struggle of all Moslem peoples with a view to safeguarding their dignity, independence, and national rights;

CALLING UPON all states to respect the sovereignty, territorial integrity, political independence, nonaligned status, and Islamic identity of Afghanistan;

REAFFIRMING the determination of the Islamic states to pursue a policy of nonalignment and to oppose superpower interference in the affairs of Islamic countries;

EXPRESSING its hope that the nonaligned movement will play an

From *New York Times*, May 23, 1980, p. A10. Official English text: Reuters.

active role in the search for a comprehensive solution to the Afghan crisis consistent with this resolution in order to strengthen peace and stability in the region and in the world and the purposes and objectives of the movement;

[The Conference of Islamic Foreign Ministers]

1. REAFFIRMS the resolution on the Soviet military intervention in Afghanistan and on its ensuing effects adopted at the extraordinary session of the Islamic Conference;

2. EXPRESSES its deep concern at the continued Soviet military presence in Afghanistan;

3. REITERATES its demand for the immediate, total, and unconditional withdrawal of all Soviet troops stationed on the territory of Afghanistan;

4. REAFFIRMS respect for the inalienable national right of the people of Afghanistan to determine their own form of government and choose their economic, political, and social system free from outside interference or coercion;

5. STRONGLY URGES the creation of the right conditions that would permit the early return of the Afghan refugees to their homeland in security and honor;

6. REITERATES its appeal to all states and peoples to provide assistance in order to alleviate the sufferings of the Afghan refugees;

7. DECIDES, in order to give effect to the provisions of this resolution, to establish a committee comprising the foreign ministers of the Islamic Republic of Iran and the Islamic Republic of Pakistan and the Secretary General of the Organization of the Islamic Conference to seek ways and means, including appropriate consultations as well as the convening of an international conference under the auspices of the United Nations or otherwise, for a comprehensive solution of the grave crisis with respect to Afghanistan, provided that it is not inconsistent with this resolution.

Notes

1. The People and Their Land

1. Richard S. Newell, *The Politics of Afghanistan* (Ithaca: Cornell University Press, 1972), pp. 5–6.

2. John F. Shroder, "Regional Distribution of Physical Resources in Afghanistan," paper presented at the Conference on Rural Afghanistan, University of Nebraska at Omaha, September 1976.

2. The Rise and Fall of the Afghan Monarchy

1. English literature on the Afghan monarchy has been enriched greatly by a number of new works in recent years. Among the most valuable have been Ludwig Adamec, *Afghanistan, 1900–1923: A Diplomatic History* (Berkeley: University of California Press, 1967) and *Afghanistan's Foreign Affairs to the Mid-Twentieth Century: Relations with Russia, Germany, and Britain* (Tucson: University of Arizona Press, 1974); Arnold Fletcher, *Afghanistan: Highway of Conquest* (Ithaca: Cornell University Press, 1965); Varton Gregorian, *The Emergence of Modern Afghanistan: Politics of Reform and Modernization, 1800–1946* (Palo Alto: Stanford University Press, 1969); Hasan Kawun Kakar, *Government and Society in Afghanistan: The Reign of Amir Abd al-Rahman Khan* (Austin: University of Texas Press, 1979); and Leon Poullada, *Reform and Rebellion in Afghanistan, 1919–1929* (Ithaca: Cornell University Press, 1973).

2. Leon Poullada, "Afghanistan and the United States: The Crucial Years," *Middle East Journal*, forthcoming.

3. Louis Duprée, "Afghanistan's Big Gamble," pts. 1–3, *American University Field Staff Reports*, South Asia Series 4, nos. 3–5 (1960) (hereafter cited as *AUFS Reports*).

4. Louis Duprée, "The Durand Line of 1893: A Case Study in Artificial Boundaries and Culture Areas," in *Current Problems in Afghanistan*

Notes

(proceedings of Princeton University Conference) (Tucson: University of Arizona Press, 1961), pp. 77–93.

5. Louis Duprée, "Pushtunistan: The Problem and Its Larger Implications," pts. 1–3, *AUFS Reports*, South Asia Series 5 (1961), and "The Decade of Daoud Ends," *AUFS Reports*, South Asia Series 7, no. 7 (1963).

6. Richard S. Newell, *The Politics of Afghanistan* (Ithaca: Cornell University Press, 1972), pp. 95–116.

7. Louis Duprée, "Constitutional Development and Cultural Change," pt. 8, *AUFS Reports*, South Asia Series 9, no. 10 (1965).

8. Newell, *Politics of Afghanistan*, pp. 162–84.

9. Ibid., pp. 150–61.

10. This estimate is based on Central Statistical Office, Government of Afghanistan, and the U.S. Agency for International Development, *National Demographic and Family Guidance Survey of the Settled Population of Afghanistan*, vol. 3 (Washington, D.C.: Government Printing Office, 1975). The figures indicate that 115,125 Afghans had at least twelve years of formal education by 1975.

11. Hanna Negaram, "Afghanistan: A Marxist Regime in a Muslim Society," *Current History* 77 (April 1979):59.

12. Louis Duprée, "Toward Representative Government in Afghanistan," pt. 1, *AUFS Reports*, 1978, Asia no. 1.

13. Theodore Eliot, "Afghanistan after the 1978 Revolution," *Strategic Review* 7, no. 1 (Spring 1979):59.

14. Hamidullah Amin and Gordon B. Schilz, *A Geography of Afghanistan* (Omaha: Center for Afghanistan Studies, University of Nebraska, 1976), p. 169.

15. Louis Duprée, "A Note on Afghanistan," *AUFS Reports*, South Asia Series 18, no. 6 (1974):9.

3. Marxism in Afghanistan

1. Richard S. Newell, "Afghanistan: The Dangers of Cold War Generosity," *Middle East Journal* 23, no. 2 (1969):168–75.

2. "Biography of the Great Leader," *Kabul Times*, October 30, 1978.

3. *New York Times*, November 12, 1953, p. 9.

4. Ibid., December 17, 1953, p. 6.

5. *Kabul Times*, October 30, 1978.

6. Personal communication from a graduate of the Kabul Teacher

Training High School who was a resident student during the time Amin was its principal.

7. Louis Duprée, "Afghanistan, 1966," *American University Field Staff Reports*, South Asia Series 10, no. 4 (1966):12–14.

4. The Khalq Regime, April 27, 1978–December 27, 1979

1. The *Kabul Times* published on account of the coup and the preparations leading up to it on October 30, 1978. It is the primary source for the description presented here.

2. Louis Duprée, "Red Flag over the Hindu Kush," pt. 2: "The Accidental Coup or Taraki in Blunderland," *American University Field Staff Reports*, 1979, Asia no. 45, p. 6 (hereafter cited as *AUFS Reports*).

3. Ibid., p. 8.

4. Ibid., p. 10.

5. *Kabul Times*, October 30, 1978.

6. Louis Duprée, "The Democratic Republic of Afghanistan, 1979: Rhetoric, Repression, Reforms and Revolts," *AUFS Reports*, 1979, Asia no. 32, p. 2.

7. *New York Times*, May 7, 1978, p. 1.

8. *Manchester Guardian*, November 5, 1978.

9. *Kabul Times*, September 23, 1978.

10. Jon W. Anderson and Richard F. Strand, eds., "Ethnic Processes and Intergroup Relations in Contemporary Afghanistan." Occasional Paper no. 15, Afghanistan Council of the Asia Society, Summer 1978.

11. Thomas J. Barfield, "The Impact of Pushtun Immigration on Nomadic Pastoralism in Northeastern Afghanistan," in ibid., pp. 26–34.

12. Asen Balikci, "The Nomadic Family in Transition," paper delivered at Conference on Rural Afghanistan, University of Nebraska at Omaha, September 1976.

13. *Korean Herald* (Seoul), May 25, 1979, as reprinted in Afghanistan Council of the Asian Society *Newsletter*, June 1979, p. 49.

14. Central Statistical Office, Government of Afghanistan, and U.S. Agency for International Development, *National Demographic and Family Guidance Survey of the Settled Population of Afghanistan* (Washington, D.C., 1975), vol. 3, Table 10.1.1, p. 59, and Table 10.1.3, p. 61.

15. *New York Times*, December 6, 1978, p. A1.

16. *Economist*, September 22, 1979, pp. 17–18.

17. *Washington Post*, July 16, 1979, p. A12.

18. *Dawn Overseas* (Karachi), April 7, 1979, as reprinted in Afghanistan Council of the Asia Society *Newsletter,* June 1979, p. 2.

19. *London Daily Telegraph,* June 3, 1979, as reprinted in Afghanistan Council of the Asia Society *Newsletter,* June 1979, p. 28.

20. *Economist,* September 22, 1979, pp. 17–18.

21. Kabul Radio, October 9, 1979.

22. *Economist,* November 3, 1979, pp. 52–53.

23. *New York Times,* January 4, 1980, p. A1; Kuldip Nayar, *Report on Afghanistan* (New Delhi: Allied Publishers, 1981), pp. 5–7, 9, 10.

5. The Resistance

1. From an interview reported in the *Korean Herald* (Seoul), March 28, 1979.

2. *Economist,* February 2, 1980, p. 49.

3. Hanna Negaram, "The Afghan Coup of April, 1978: Revolution and International Security," *Orbis* 22, no. 2 (1979):103.

4. Richard F. Strand, "Tribal Government vs. Official Government in Nuristan: Implications for Development," paper delivered at Conference on Rural Afghanistan, University of Nebraska at Omaha, September 1976.

5. Declaration of the Afghanistan National Liberation Front, as released to the press December 8, 1978.

6. David Chaffetz, "Afghanistan, Russia's Vietnam?," Special Paper no. 4, Afghanistan Council of the Asia Society, p. 6.

6. The Soviet Invasion of December 1979

1. *New York Times,* January 1, 1980, p. 1.

2. Tass, as reported in *Des Moines Register,* January 4, 1980, p. 1A.

3. *Pravda,* as reported in *Des Moines Register,* December 31, 1979, p. 8A.

4. *New York Times,* December 28, 1979, p. A1.

5. Ibid.

6. Mohan Ram, in *Far Eastern Economic Review,* January 25, 1980.

7. *New York Times,* December 30, 1979, p. 1.

8. *Washington Post,* January 25, 1980, p. A20.

9. Mohan Ram, in *Far Eastern Economic Review,* January 25, 1980.

10. *Economist,* May 10, 1980, p. 35.

11. *Economist,* August 2, 1980, p. 34.

12. *Washington Post,* January 5, 1980, p. A1; *New York Times,* March 13, 1980, p. A3.

13. *Kabul New Times,* January 1, 1980; italics added.

14. *Christian Science Monitor,* May 12, 1980, p. 3.

7. The Struggle for Afghanistan

1. Nancy Lubin, "The Mullah and the Commissar," *Geo,* June 1980, p. 16.

2. *Christian Science Monitor,* March 4, 1981, p. 1.

3. *New York Times,* January 8, 1980, p. A6.

4. Ibid., January 10, 1980, p. A1.

5. *Des Moines Register,* January 22, 1980, p. 2A.

6. Associated Press, as published in *Des Moines Register,* March 11, 1980, p. 2A.

7. *Washington Post,* August 10, 1980, p. A22.

8. *Newsweek,* May 26, 1980, pp. 46–47.

9. *Asiaweek,* May 16, 1980, pp. 25, 26.

10. *Pravda,* as reported in *Des Moines Register,* June 6, 1980, p. 2A.

11. *Far Eastern Economic Review,* April 18, 1980, p. 25.

12. *Time,* April 7, 1980, pp. 40–43.

13. *Asiaweek,* May 30, 1980, p. 12.

14. M. Afzal Khan, "With the Afghan Rebels," *New York Times Magazine,* January 13, 1980. © 1980 by The New York Times Company. Reprinted by permission.

15. Reprinted by permission from *The Christian Science Monitor,* June 2, 1980, p. 14. © 1980 by The Christian Science Publishing Society. All rights reserved.

16. *Asiaweek,* May 30, 1980, p. 13.

17. *Newsweek,* March 24, 1980, pp. 57–60.

18. Associated Press, as published in *Des Moines Register,* June 1, 1980, p. 3A.

19. *New York Times,* March 7, 1980, p. A8.

20. *Suddeutshe Zeitung,* January 25, 1980, as reprinted in *World Press Review,* April 1980, p. 58.

21. *Christian Science Monitor,* January 2, 1980, p. 7.

22. *Newsweek,* January 14, 1980, pp. 24–27.

23. *World Press Review,* July 1980, p. 26.

24. *Time,* April 28, 1980, p. 31.

25. *Christian Science Monitor,* May 28, 1980, p. 1.

Notes

26. *Des Moines Register*, April 18, 1980.
27. *Time*, April 14, 1980, p. 56.
28. *Asiaweek*, May 16, 1980, p. 25.
29. Ibid., May 30, 1980, pp. 26, 31.
30. Ibid., p. 12.
31. *Wall Street Journal*, January 23, 1980, p. 1.
32. *Washington Post*, August 11, 1980, p. A1; *Des Moines Register*, August 8, 1980, p. 4A, and August 18, 1980, p. 2A.
33. Associated Press, as published in *Des Moines Register*, June 1, 1980, p. 3A.
34. *Dawn Overseas* (Karachi), March 15, 1980.
35. Eric Abraham, *The Listener*, April 3, 1980, p. 432.
36. United Press International, as published in *Cedar Falls Record*, January 25, 1980, p. 2.
37. *Economist*, February 16, 1980, pp. 38–43.
38. *Des Moines Register*, April 7, 1980, p. 2A.
39. *Time*, April 28, 1980, p. 31; Associated Press, as published in *Des Moines Register*, May 24, 1980, p. 2A.
40. Associated Press, as published in *Des Moines Register*, June 7, 1980, p. 2A; June 8, 1980, p. 3A; June 10, 1980, p. 2A.
41. Ibid., September 8, 1980, p. 2A.
42. *Christian Science Monitor*, January 21, 1980, p. 1.
43. *Wall Street Journal*, January 23, p. 1; *Washington Post*, February 8, 1980, p. A20.
44. *New York Times*, February 23, 1980, p. 1.
45. Numerous accounts have been published. See *Los Angeles Times*, February 25, 1980; *New York Times*, February 23–28, 1980; *Newsweek*, March 3, 1980, pp. 24–25, and March 10, 1980, pp. 57–60.
46. *Christian Science Monitor*, April 15, 1980, p. 1.
47. Personal communication from an eyewitness.
48. *Newsweek*, April 14, 1980, p. 48.
49. The most detailed accounts of student protests appeared in *World Press Review*, July 1980, p. 26; *Korean Herald* (Seoul), May 30, 1980; and *New York Times*, May 11, 1980, p. 3.
50. *Des Moines Register*, June 13, 1980, p. 5A.
51. Ibid.
52. *Time*, January 14, 1980, pp. 10–17; *Newsweek*, January 14, 1980, pp. 24–27.
53. *Economist*, August 2, 1980, p. 34; Associated Press, as reported in *Des Moines Register*, August 2, 1980, p. 2A, and August 4, 1980, p. 2A.

226

54. *Christian Science Monitor*, May 9, 1980, p. 5, and May 14, 1980, p. 1.

55. *Time*, January 14, 1980, pp. 10–17.

56. *Des Moines Register*, March 5, 1980, p. 2A.

57. *Korean Herald*, February 11, 1980, as reprinted in Afghanistan Council of the Asia Society *Newsletter*, March 1980, p. 7.

58. *Washington Post*, February 15, 1980, p. A1.

59. *Christian Science Monitor*, February 14, 1980, p. 1.

60. *New York Times*, May 23, 1980, p. A10.

8. A New Era of Crisis

1. *New York Times*, August 3, 1979, pp. A1, A5.

2. *Dawn Overseas* (Karachi), October 6, 1979, as reprinted in Afghanistan Council of the Asia Society *Newsletter*, January 1980, p. 18.

3. *Christian Science Monitor*, January 4, 1980, p. 1.

4. In his well-informed account of the Afghanistan crisis, Kuldip Nayar claims that the January meeting of the Islamic Conference was called after Lord Carrington, the British foreign secretary, persuaded the Saudi Arabian government to sponsor it *(Report on Afghanistan* [New Delhi: Allied Publishers, 1981], pp. 60–61).

Index

Abraham, Eric, 163
Afghan Construction Unit, 56
Afghanistan, Democratic Republic of
  (DRA), 72, 85, 124; Fundamental
  Principles of, 125. See also Khalq
  government; Parcham government.
Afghanistan, Republic of (July
  1973–April 1978), 45–47, 52, 57,
  64, 67–70, 73, 75, 94–96, 100, 111,
  123
Afghan monarchy. See Royal family.
Afghan National Liberation Front,
  182, 183
Africa, 116–17
Agriculture, 23, 26, 28–30, 42, 48, 80,
  127, 136
Agriculture, Ministry of, 123
Ahmadzai, Shapur, 75
Air attacks: on Herat, 85; on Paktia,
  159
Air Force, Afghan, 31, 37, 42, 69, 87,
  89, 176
Alexander the Great, 23, 98
Ali, Amir, 35
Amanullah Shah, 37–41, 93, 110, 184
Amin, Asadullah, 90
Amin, Hafizullah, 60–62, 64, 66–69,
  71–75, 78, 87–90, 105–8, 114, 115,
  118–24, 129, 132, 174, 178;
  government of, 113, 159
Amu Darya (Oxus) River, 25, 27, 28,
  107
Angola, 117, 152
Ariana (Afghan national airline), 56

Army, Afghan, 39, 41–42, 71, 85–89,
  100, 106, 109–10, 112–13, 123,
  154, 170, 172, 176, 178, 180–81;
  assisted by USSR, 41–42, 46, 64, 74,
  111–12, 114, 178; attacks Soviet
  units and personnel, 145, 155, 159,
  178–80; collaborates with
  resistance, 145, 158, 179, 180;
  conscription and recruitment for,
  39, 89, 126, 181; defections and
  mutinies in, 85–87, 89, 106, 119,
  129, 131–32, 140, 145–47, 153–55,
  158–59, 163, 172, 176, 179–81;
  deployment of, by Soviets, 134,
  136, 176, 180; factionalism in, 176;
  4th Armored Division, 69–70; 14th
  Armored Division, 123, 180; Kunar
  garrison, 155, 158; officer training,
  42; Rishkor Division, 70
Auerbach, Stuart, 137–38
Azerbaijan Turks, 118
Azim, Muhammad Ibrahim, 123

Babrakzai, Muhammad, 184
Bactrian Plains, 28
Badakhshan, 91, 96, 101, 131, 138,
  144–45, 153–54, 179
Baghlan: city, 127, 154, 171, 173;
  province, 141, 154
Baluch, 25; of Iran, 118; language of,
  74; of Pakistan, 118; and resistance,
  91, 95
Baluchistan, Pakistan, 27, 29
Bamiyan, 30, 102, 145, 153, 163, 180

229

Index

Bangladesh War, 204
Banking, 39, 47, 50–51, 54, 78
Barikot, 155
Baryalay, Muhammad, 122
Begram Air Base, 31, 69–70, 163, 178–79
Bhutto, Zulfikar Ali, 49
Bolsheviks, 25, 37, 110
Brezhnev, Leonid, 88, 180, 194
Brezhnev Doctrine, 48, 108
British Empire, 34–39, 41, 43, 99, 109. *See also* Great Britain.
Brzezinski, Zbigniew, 196
Bureaucracy, 47, 53–54, 63, 74
Bureaucrats, 73, 78; attacks against, 85, 91; rural, 83–84, 91, 98–99, 141, 162; Russian replacements of, 120
Buzkashi, 25

Came, Barry, 144
Camp David Accords, 197
Carter, Jimmy, 193; administration of, 192, 203
—responses of, to Soviet invasion of Afghanistan, 192–95, 201–2, 211–12; draft registration, 193; grain embargo, 192–93; Middle East bases, 201–3, 211; Olympic Games boycott, 193–94
Carter Doctrine, 194–95
Casualties: Afghan civilian, 85, 104, 136–39, 147–48, 157, 172–75, 188; among Marxist officials, 131, 172; among Soviets in Afghanistan, 131, 134, 137, 152–53, 167
Central Asia, 36, 37, 101, 110, 152; troops from, 132
Central Intelligence Agency, 188
Chigha Sarai, 100, 136, 158
Children in Afghan resistance, 151, 173
China, 56, 77, 115, 152, 187, 205, 210; and United States, 116
Cities, resistance in, 170–74, 183
Civil rights, 44, 47
Climate, 26, 28, 131, 134, 149
Commerce. *See* Trade.
Commerce, Ministry of, 55, 123

Communications, Ministry of, 70
Constitutional government. *See* Zahir Shah, liberal government under.
Constitutions: Amanullah's (1923), 37; Daoud's (1977), 47; Zahir Shah's (1964), 44, 62, 123
Coups: July 1973, 46, 63–65
—April 1978, 64, 66–72, 107, 112, 121; anniversary celebrations of, 125, 173–74; international reaction to, 195; Soviet involvement in, 113
—September 1979, 88
Credit, 75, 81
Cuba, 88, 116, 117, 152

Danish, Muhammad Ismail, 120
Daoud, Muhammad, 34, 42–46, 53, 59–60, 62–65, 67–70, 93–94, 96, 100, 110–13; death of, 52, 70–71, 105; diplomacy of, 49–51; and purge of Parcham, 47–48; reforms of, 47. *See also* Afghanistan, Republic of.
Dari, 25, 62
Darulaman palace, 90
Development programs, 42, 45, 47, 48
De Voss, David, 157
Dhofar Rebellion, 117
Dost Muhammad, 35
Dubs, Adolph, 105, 196
Durand Line, 43
Durrani, Ahmad Shah, 35
Durrani tribe, 73, 159

East Europe, 54, 89, 115, 152; advisers from, 119
East Germany, 119
Economic policies: Khalq, 78–80; Parcham, 125, 127
Economy, 22, 36, 39, 41, 42, 45, 47. *See also* Development programs.
Educated middle class, 39, 40, 43–44, 92, 94, 111, 119, 175–76; unemployment among, 48, 54
Education, 35, 37, 40, 42, 44, 92, 125, 126, 175; foreign assistance to, 56–58; foreign influence in, 35, 37–40, 53–56, 175

Education, Ministry of, 70, 174
Educational reforms: of Amanullah,
37–38; of Daoud, 42, 47; of Khalq,
75, 83; of Parcham, 125–27, 175,
176
Egypt, 50, 55, 116, 188, 195, 197, 200
Enver Pasha, 37
Ethics, 22, 23, 80
Ethiopia, 117, 152

Faizabad, 30, 101, 145, 154; airport,
145, 159, 179
Family, Afghan, 78–80, 82–84
Farah, 30, 153, 161
Farhadi, Rawan, 123
Farhang, Muhammad Siddiq, 123
Farmers, 23, 25–30, 78–81, 136–37
Fisk, Robert, 132
Flag, Afghan national, 55, 76, 84–85,
103, 122, 125, 174
Foreign affairs, Afghan, 35–37, 50,
51, 56
Foreign Affairs, Ministry of, 70
Foreign aid, 40–42, 45–46, 49–51, 56
Foreign policy: of Daoud's republic,
49–50; of Democratic Republic,
200; royal, 35–37, 40–41
France, 37, 38, 55
Freedom fighters. See Resistance.
Friendship treaties with Soviet Union:
Amanullah's, 37; Khalq's, 85, 103,
196
Frontier Affairs, Ministry of, 46–47

Gailani, Hasan, 143
Gailani, Sayyid Ahmed Effendi, 94,
103, 145, 151, 183–84, 189
Gandhi, Indira, 205
Genghis Khan, 102
Geography, 26–28
Germany, 39, 40, 55, 56
Ghazni, 30, 59, 123, 138, 159, 180
Ghilzai tribe, 59, 73, 159
Girardet, Edward, 143–44, 188–89
Girishk, 159
Grand Mosque of Mecca, 117
Great Britain, 41, 60. See also British
Empire.
Gujars, 100

Gulabzoi, Sayyid Muhammad, 120,
122–23
Gwadar, 49

Habibiya High School, 174
Habibullah, Amir, 36, 105
Hajigak iron deposit, 49
Hazarajat, 101–2, 153, 162–63
Hazaras, 25, 35, 101–2, 130, 173; in
Kabul, 92, 173; in resistance, 96,
103, 162–63
Hazrat Sahib of Shor Bazaar, Kabul,
93, 104
Hekmatyar, Gulbuddin, 48, 94–95,
183, 189
Helmand River, 28, 49
Herat, 30, 85–86, 105, 127, 145, 147,
153, 161–62, 173, 179; Shias in, 92;
uprisings in, 85–86, 171
Hizb-i-Islami (Islamic Party), 94–95,
145, 151, 154, 159, 161, 182–85; in
Kandahar, 141, 144; in Kama
District, Nangarhar, 144
Households. See Family, Afghan.
Howe, Marvine, 189
Hussein, Mengal, 151
Hydroelectric power, 30, 36

Ihlau, Olaf, 149
Ikwan-i-Musalamin (Islamic
Brotherhood), 48, 77, 94–96, 98,
183
India: nationalism in, 37; plains
region of, 29, 36; press in, 130–31;
reaction of, to Soviet invasion of
Afghanistan, 205–6; and United
States, 197, 202, 204–5
Indus River, 23, 28, 29
Insurgents. See Mujahidin;
Resistance.
Interior, Ministry of, 70, 122, 123,
174
Internal security, 36, 39, 41, 47–48,
57, 67–70, 76, 141, 146, 168, 170
International reaction to Soviet
invasion of Afghanistan, 115–16,
130, 136, 147, 196, 199, 201–2,
205–8
International Red Cross, 124

Index

Iran, 118, 145, 161, 183, 187, 192, 195, 203; Afghan migrant workers in, 50, 86; and Afghan resistance, 187–88, 210–11; Baluch region of, 25; and hostage crisis, 116, 197, 202, 212; relations of, with Afghanistan, 49, 77, 86, 113; relations of, with United States, 197–98, 211–12; revolution of 1979, 95, 198

Iraq, 50, 51, 53, 94, 117–18, 195, 203

Irrigation, 22–23, 101

Islam, 22–23, 25, 36–38, 47–48, 55, 58, 66, 72, 74, 77, 81, 95, 98, 103–5, 125, 149, 151, 191–92; revival of, 198–99, 213. *See also* Shias; Sunnis.

Islamabad, Pakistan, 183

Islamic Conference, 183, 189, 192, 199–200, 211; emergency meeting of (January 1980), 183, 199; foreign ministers' meeting (May 1980), 183, 199–200

Islamic leaders, Afghan, 36, 38, 58, 66, 77, 104–5, 125

Islamic Revolutionary Front, 94, 182, 189

Islamic Revolutionary Movement, 95

Israel, 195, 197, 199, 200, 203–4, 211

Jalalabad, 30, 86, 139, 143–45, 155, 157, 171, 173; army mutinies in, 155, 178–79; insurgent assault in (May 1979), 56

Jalalar, Muhammad Khan, 123

Jamiyat-i-Islami, 95, 145, 154, 182–85; of Pakistan, 95

Justice, Ministry of, 55

Kabul, 29–30, 37–38, 45, 48, 56, 60–63, 69–71, 78, 87, 89, 102, 106, 108, 163; airport, 69; army mutiny in (April 1980), 179–80; Bala Hissar, 87, 106; foreign residents of, 47; Kargha sector, 167; mujahid threats to, 144, 167; resistance and uprisings in, 87, 89, 106, 108, 135, 141, 172, 198

Kabul Hotel, 105

Kabul University, 47, 54, 174; foreign influences on, 55, 62

Kama District, Nangarhar, 144, 158

Kandahar, 28–30, 86, 127, 141, 173, 179; airport, 31; uprisings in, 170–71, 173

Kandahar–Herat highway, 134, 161

Kandahar–Kabul highway, 134, 159

Kargha Barracks, Kabul, 172, 179

Karmal, Babrak, 23, 62–63, 67, 71–74, 88, 108, 118–21, 123–25, 129, 172, 180

Keshtmand, Ali Sultan, 75

Keshtmand, Asadullah, 122

Khadafy, Muammar, 198–99

Khalq government, 63, 66–68, 71–72, 81, 85–88, 90–91, 94, 102–3, 106–8, 110, 114, 124, 147; cabinet of, 72; minorities policy of, 74–75; other policies of, 72–77, 81–85, 103, 113, 121; propaganda of, 77–78, 80–81, 86, 105; reorganization of, 86–89; and struggle with Parcham, 72–75, 87, 122; and suppression of opposition, 77, 89, 100, 104, 106, 147; and USSR, 62

Khalq party, 52, 60, 62–68, 71–75, 78, 96, 113, 120, 176, 180; officials of, 76; and preparations for April 1978 coup, 66–68; and student agitation, 174; and USSR, 62, 72, 75

Khan, Afzal, 142

Khomeini, Ayatollah Ruhollah, 86, 192

Khulm, 162

Khyber, Mir Akbar, 62, 68

Khyber Pass, 29, 30, 134; highway to Kabul, 155

Kohdaman Valley, 87, 163, 167

Kunar Province, 157–59, 182

Kunar Valley, 98, 100, 135, 136, 138, 145, 153, 155; Soviet offensive in, 157–58, 179

Kunduz, 29, 30, 159

Kuwait, 50, 51

Kwitney, Jonathan, 162
Kyrala (Kerala) massacre, 147

Laghman, 135–36, 157, 159
Land tenure, 79–83
Languages, 19, 25, 132, 185; Dari, 25, 62; influence of Western European, on education, 37; minority, policy on, 74–75, 162; Pushtu, 25; Russian, 75, 83, 126
Leadership, local, 35, 38–39, 48, 80–81, 98–99
Lee, David, 173
Libya, 198–99
Logar Province, 163, 166
Logar Valley, 87, 167
Loya jirgah, 44, 125, 184; momaselu, 184–85, 212

Maiwandwal, Muhammad Hashim, 96
Marriage, 75, 79; reforms in, 81, 83, 125
Marxists in Afghanistan, 34, 45–46, 53, 55, 58–65, 95, 111–12; origins of, 58–59; rise of, through educational dissent, 56–58
Maududi, Maulana, 95
Mazar-i-Sharif, 30, 86, 134, 153, 162
Mazduryar, Sherjan, 122
Mecca, 53, 117
Media. See Press.
Middle class. See Educated middle class.
Middle East, 52, 53, 190–92, 195–96, 201, 203–4; bilateral aid to, 190–91; interstate conflicts in, 198–99, 211; political instability of, 191, 198
Military officers: in government, 122–23, 175, 178
—in politics: Khalq, 67–69, 72; Parcham, 63–64, 125–26, 134, 136, 175, 178
Minerals, 31, 49
Mines and Industries, Ministry of, 55
Ministries, 46, 55, 120. See also names of specific ministries.
Minorities, Khalq policy on, 74–75

MI-24 gunships, 87, 139, 141–42, 157, 185
Mohmand, Fazal Rahim 123
Mongolia, 48, 109, 120, 123
Muhammad Reza Pahlavi, shah of Iran, 49, 197–98, 203
Mujadidi, Sibghatullah, 93–94, 183–84
Mujadidi family, 93, 103–4
Mujahidin: effectiveness of, 141–45, 154, 158, 161, 182; military equipment of, 140–44, 158, 161, 185–87; tactics of, 140–44, 146–47, 151, 155, 157–58, 161, 167; territorial and political rivalries of, 141, 145, 182–85. See also Resistance.
Mullahs. See Islamic leaders.
Musahiban family, 38–39, 93
Muslim bloc, 111, 115, 118, 183, 188, 201; and OPEC aid to Afghanistan, 45; pressure on Daoud government from, 49–50; support for Afghan resistance from, 92, 211

Nabi, Malawi Muhammad, 95
Nadir Khan (later shah), 38, 184
Naim, Muhammad, 71
Nakshbandi order, 93
Nangarhar, 135–36, 138, 155, 157
National Revolutionary Party of Daoud, 49
Neutrality proposal, 200
New Model Revolution, 124
Niazi, Muhammad, 48, 95–96
Nomads, 22, 23, 25, 28–30, 78–79, 101
Nuristani, Abdul Qadir, 68
Nuristanis (Kafirs), 25, 35, 91, 96, 98–100, 103, 130, 158–59, 187

Olympic Games, 193–94, 199, 205
OPEC nations, 45, 50
Opium, 157

Pacification policies, 129–31, 135–36, 138–40, 151–52, 155, 162, 176, 178, 180, 191, 194

Index

Paghman, 60, 167
Pakistan, 40, 41, 77, 192, 197; and
    Afghanistan, 43, 113; and press,
    130; as source of weapons for
    Afghan resistance, 187–89, 200,
    210–11, 213; and United States,
    197, 202, 204–5, 211–12. *See also*
    Refugees.
Paktia, 94, 106, 143, 153, 159
Palace guards, 69–70, 88
Palestine Liberation Organization
    (PLO), 199
Palestinians, 116, 199, 204
Pan American Airways, 56
Panjshir Valley, 94, 145; Soviet attack
    on, 167
Panjshiri, Dastagir, 120
Paputin, Viktor S., 90, 114
Parcham government, 118–29,
    146–47, 153, 200; factionalism in,
    119–24, 174–75, 180; internal
    support for, 119–20, 127, 162, 173,
    175–76; militia of, 126, 168, 170,
    173; policies of, 121, 123–26;
    propaganda of, 109, 119, 121,
    130–31, 173–74, 188
Parcham party, 46–49, 52–53, 62–66,
    72–73, 75, 96, 107, 111–12, 114,
    125; central committee of, 120;
    officials of, 120, 122–23; and Soviet
    Union, 66–68, 71–72, 74, 87, 113
Parliament (National Assembly,
    Wolesi Jirgah), 35, 44, 59, 63, 184
Parwan, 163, 166
Patronage, 54
Paul, Anthony, 139, 161
People's Democratic Party of
    Afghanistan (PDPA), 46, 52–53, 60,
    62, 72. *See also* Khalq party;
    Parcham party.
Persian Gulf, 50, 53, 93, 117–18,
    189–90, 195, 197, 207; United
    States attempts to obtain bases in,
    200, 202–4
Petroleum and natural gas, 30–31,
    50, 56, 116, 118, 197, 207; pipeline
    broken by resistance, 162
Phosgene oxide, 138
Pich Valley, 144, 158

Planning, Ministry of, 55
Political prisoners, 121, 124, 173
Polo, Marco, 28
Population, 31
Press, 44, 62–63, 95, 130, 153–54,
    163, 178
Propaganda, 130; of Khalq
    government, 77–78, 80–81, 86,
    105; of Parcham government, 109,
    119, 121, 130–31, 173–74, 188; of
    resistance groups, 130, 153, 159; of
    Soviet Union, 108–10, 131, 134,
    139–40, 173, 188
Public Health, Ministry of, 55, 123
Puli Charkhi, 69, 86, 123, 173, 180
Pul-i-Khumri, 86
Pushtunistan issue, 42–43, 49
Pushtuns, 19, 23, 35–38, 41–43, 59,
    78–79, 89, 91–92, 94, 100–103,
    105, 118, 136, 143, 153, 155, 195

Qadir, Abdul, 69, 75–76, 122–23

Rabani, Burhanuddin, 48, 95, 183,
    188
Radio Kabul, 119, 130, 173, 178
Rafi, Muhammad, 75
Rahman, Abdur, 35–36, 43
Rasuli, Ghulam Haider, 70
Ratebzad, Dr. Anahita, 174
Reagan, Ronald, 201
Reforms, 40, 44, 47–48, 74–77, 81,
    83, 88, 103, 113, 121; of
    Amanullah, 37–38; of Daoud's
    republic, 47; of Khalq, 74–77; of
    Musahibans, 40; of Parcham, 125;
    of Zahir Shah, 44
Refugees, 106, 136–39, 148–49, 154,
    157, 199, 202, 212
Religion. *See* Islam; Nakshbandi
    order.
Resistance, 48, 77, 86–89, 91–94, 96,
    101, 103–6, 113–16, 119, 126–31,
    134, 138–45, 149, 151, 153–54,
    157–59, 161–63, 166–67, 182–85,
    187–89, 192, 208–10, 214; in cities,
    125–26, 135, 167–68, 170; opera-
    tional organization of, 92, 93, 144–
    45, 159, 183–85, 189; outside aid

Resistance (*cont.*)
to, 109, 130, 140, 182, 183, 185,
187–89, 202, 209–13
Roads and highways, 31, 33, 36, 89;
resistance interference with,
134–35, 154–55, 157, 159, 166;
Soviet construction of, 47; Soviet
use of, 107, 112, 154
Rokha, 167
Royal family, 22, 30, 34–35, 37–38,
40–41, 43, 46, 54, 57, 62–63, 73,
78, 95, 99; and government of, 39,
53
Russian Empire, 34–37
Russians in Afghanistan: and Asian
troops, 132; as objects of terror,
146–47, 170. *See also* Soviet Union.

Sadat, Anwar, 116, 188
Salang Pass, 31, 134, 166, 167
SALT II Treaty, 116, 193, 194
Saquo, Bacha, 38
Sarwari, Asadullah, 120, 122, 123
Saudi Arabia, 50, 51, 93, 117, 192,
197, 198, 203, 204
Saunders, Harold, 196
Sayef, Abdul, 183
Schools, 38, 55, 73, 83–84
Shabnamas (night letters), 172, 173
Shafiq, Mussa, 63
Shaw, John, 141
Shias, 22, 25, 92, 102, 105, 198
Shibarghan, 30
Shindand Air Base, 31, 70, 161, 162
Shola Jowid party, 95
Sistan, 27, 28, 161
Social change, 37, 40, 43, 45–47, 56,
78
Society, 19, 20, 47, 78–81, 91, 110
Somalia, 117, 203
Soman, 138
Soraya, Queen, 38
South Yemen, 117, 152
Soviet embassy, Kabul, 172, 174
Soviet Union, 37–41
—advisers in Afghanistan: attacks
against, 85, 170; civilian, 55–56, 60,
86–87, 119–20, 126–27; military,

42, 46, 64, 89, 106, 111–12, 147,
158, 178, 180
—aid to Afghanistan: economic, 42,
46, 49, 110–13, 125–26; military,
41–42, 46, 87
—and attitudes toward Afghans, 126,
157; economy of, 152
—invasion of Afghanistan by, 66,
107, 109–10, 116, 125, 129, 131,
190–95, 197, 199, 205; planning of,
107–9, 115–16, 121, 131–32, 134,
141; popular Soviet reaction to, 152
—military forces of, 107–10, 129–34,
137, 139, 143–44, 148, 151–57,
159, 161–63, 167–68, 172, 174,
178, 180, 182, 189; armored,
134–35, 137, 147, 154, 157, 161,
167; casualties, 131, 134, 137,
152–53, 167; 105th Parachute
Division, 132; tactics, 127, 130-40,
147, 149, 154, 166–68, 172, 208;
troops in Afghanistan, 86, 107,
109, 110, 134–35, 151–52, 157,
159, 162, 168, 172, 178, 182; use of
poison gas and napalm, 136–39,
154
—policy of: on Afghanistan, 111–16,
119, 128, 151–52, 185, 190, 200,
206, 208–10, 213; on Middle East,
190–91, 198–99, 207
—relations of: with Afghanistan,
40–42, 49–50, 107, 109–13, 152;
with Khalq government under
Amin, 89–90, 106–8, 114–15; with
Khalq government under Taraki,
72, 74–75, 85–89, 103, 105; with
India, 205; with Parcham
government, 108, 119–20, 123,
125, 128
—southern strategy of, 52–53,
116–18
—*See also* Bolsheviks; Russian
Empire; Russians in Afghanistan.
Soviet bloc, 103, 191, 195–96
Spin Baldak Air Base, 161
Stalin, Josef, 39, 110
Students, 38, 44, 47, 57–59, 62, 65,
73, 83–84, 89, 127, 170, 173–76
Sukhrud, 139

Index

Sunnis, 22, 119, 199
Supreme Court of Afghanistan, 44
Switzerland, 211
Syria, 117–18, 195

Tajiks, 25, 78–79, 105, 153;
 mountain, 101, 103, 154
Takhar, 101, 131, 138, 144, 154
Taraki, Nur Muhammad, 59–60, 62,
 64, 67–68, 71–74, 78, 87–88, 96,
 105, 108, 114, 119–20, 122–23; and
 coup against Amin, 88; death of, 89
Tass (Soviet news agency), 118, 200
Teachers, 37, 42, 47–48, 61, 83–84,
 126–27, 146
Telecommunications, 31, 56
Termez, USSR, 31, 132
Third World, 40, 92, 115
Third World Conference, Budapest,
 75
Trade, 36, 39, 48, 50, 54, 78, 125,
 127
Turkomans, 25, 74–75, 101, 118, 130
Turks, 37, 118

United Nations, 56; General
 Assembly resolution on invasion,
 205, 213; Russian employees of,
 killed in Kandahar, 170
United Nations Relief Agency, 212
United States: and aid to
 Afghanistan, 41–42, 51, 55–56,
 59–60, 105; and influence on
 Afghan education, 55–56, 59, 61,
 77; intelligence analysis, 107, 152,
 153
—policy of: on Afghanistan, 207,
 208; on Iran, 197–98; on Middle
 East, 197–203, 211–12; on Soviet
 Union, 192–97, 201–3, 208,
 211–14
—prospects for military aid to
 Afghan resistance, 188
—relations of: with Afghanistan,
 41–42, 105, 110; with China, 116;
 with India, 197, 202, 204–5; with
 Pakistan, 197, 202, 205, 211–12;
 with Soviet Union, 107, 116, 152,
 192, 194–96, 198, 201
—See also Carter, Jimmy; Carter
 Doctrine; Central Intelligence
 Agency.
U.S. embassy, Kabul, 60, 105
U.S. Navy, 200
U.S. Senate, 116, 193
USSR. See Soviet Union.
Uzbeks, 25, 35, 74–75, 78–79, 96,
 101, 154; and resistance, 130, 153

Vietnam, 138, 152
Vietnam War, 202
Voice of America, 202

Wakhan Corridor, 28
Wali, Abdul, 64
Wardak, 94, 173
Watanjar, Muhammad Aslam, 69–71,
 122–23
Western Europe, 116, 192, 194,
 200–201
Women, 25, 38, 39, 83; in
 demonstrations, 174–76; among
 refugees, 149, 157; in resistance,
 151, 167
World War I, 37, 139
World War II, 39–40

Youth, as security agents in Kabul,
 170
Youth for Reform, 59

Zafarruddin, guerrilla commander,
 161
Zahir Shah, 34, 42, 43, 46, 63–65,
 111–12, 184; liberal government
 under, 43–45, 54, 58, 62–65, 84,
 111, 112, 123
Zeari, Saleh Muhammad, 120
Zia-ul-Haq, Muhammad, 188
Zimyanin, Mikhail, 174